LAURENCE BOSWELL

Laurence Boswell read Drama at Manchester University before working as a freelance director in various regional theatres. As Artistic Director of the Gate Theatre, London (1991-96), he directed numerous productions including the Spanish Golden Age Season, which won the 1993 Oliver Award for Outstanding Achievement. In the West End he has directed Ben Elton's *Popcorn*, Kenneth Lonergan's *This is our Youth*, David Williamson's *Up for Grabs* and Peter Nichols's *A Day in the Death of Joe Egg*, receiving a Tony Award nomination for Best Director when it transferred to Broadway.

He is currently director of Laurence Boswell Productions, a subsidiary of ATG, and an Associate Director of the Royal Shakespeare Company, where he is preparing a season of plays from the Golden Age to be presented in the Swan Theate in summer 2004.

Other title in this series

Anon
THE MYSTERIES

Patrick Barlow
LOVE UPON THE THRONE
THE MESSIAH

John Clifford
LIGHT IN THE VILLAGE

Dominic Cooke
ARABIAN NIGHTS

Helen Edmundson
ANNA KARENINA
THE CLEARING
THE MILL ON THE FLOSS
WAR AND PEACE

Heimann/ Monaghan/ Petterle
100

Barry Hines / Lawrence Till
KES

Ayub Khan-Din
EAST IS EAST

Mike Leigh
ECSTACY
SMELLING A RAT

Liz Lochhead
MEDEA
MISERYGUTS & TARTUFFE
PERFECT DAYS
THEBANS

Luscombe & McKee
THE SHAKESPEARE REVUE

Clare McIntyre
MY HEART'S A SUITCASE & LOW LEVEL PANIC
THE MATHS TUTOR
THE THICKNESS OF SKIN

Conor McPherson
DUBLIN CAROL
MCPHERSON: FOUR PLAYS
PORT AUTHORITY
THE WEIR

Miller & MacKichan
EMMA

Rufus Norris
SLEEPING BEAUTY

Stuart Paterson
CINDERELLA
HANSEL AND GRETEL

Terence Rattigan
THE BROWNING VERSION
FRENCH WITHOUT TEARS
THE WINSLOW BOY

Edmond Rostand,
trans. Antony Burgess
CYRANO DE BERGERAC

Diane Samuels
KINDERTRANSPORT

Polly Teale
AFTER MRS ROCHESTER
JANE EYRE *after* Charlotte Brontë

Sophie Treadwell
MACHINAL

Paul Webb
FOUR NIGHTS IN KNARESBOROUGH

Fay Weldon
MADAME BOVARY - BREAKFAST WITH EMMA *after* Flaubert

Amanda Whittington
BE MY BABY

Nicholas Wright
HIS DARK MATERIALS *after* Phillip Pullman

Laurence Boswell

BEAUTY AND THE BEAST

NICK HERN BOOKS
London
www.nickhernbooks.co.uk

A Nick Hern Book

This edition of *Beauty and the Beast* first published in 2003
as an original paperback by Nick Hern Books Limited, 14 Larden Road,
London W3 7ST, in association with the Royal Shakespeare Company

Beauty's speech on p.77–78 is taken from William Blake's 'The Lamb',
Songs of Innocence and Experience

Typeset by Country Setting, Kingsdown, Kent CT14 8ES
Printed and bound in Great Britain by Biddles of Guildford

A CIP catalogue record for this book is available from the British Library

ISBN 185459 769 8

BEAUTY AND THE BEAST

THE ROYAL SHAKESPEARE COMPANY

The Royal Shakespeare Company is one of the world's best-known theatre ensembles.

The Company is widely regarded as one of the most important interpreters of Shakespeare and other dramatists. Today the RSC is at the leading edge of classical theatre, with an international reputation for artistic excellence, accessibility and high quality live performance.

Our aim is to create outstanding theatre relevant to our times through the work of Shakespeare, other Renaissance dramatists, international and contemporary writers. Over the past five years the RSC has successfully staged family shows in the Royal Shakespeare Theatre. *Beauty and the Beast* continues this tradition of encouraging theatre going among young people.

We want to give as many people as possible, from all walks of life, a richer understanding and enjoyment of language and theatre. Through education and outreach programmes we continually strive to engage people with the experience of live performance.

We perform throughout the year at our home in Stratford-upon-Avon and that work is complemented by a presence in other areas of the UK. We play regularly in London, at an annual residency in Newcastle upon Tyne and many of our productions visit major regional theatres around Britain. In addition, our mobile auditorium tour sets up in community centres, sports halls and schools in areas throughout the UK with little access to professional theatre.

While the UK is the home of our Company,
our audiences are global. We regularly play to theatregoers in other parts of Europe, across the United States, the Americas, Asia and Australasia and we are proud of our relationships with partnering organisations throughout the world.

The RSC is at heart an ensemble Company. The continuation of this great tradition informs the work of all members of the Company. Directors, actors, dramatists and theatre practitioners all collaborate in the creation of the RSC's distinctive and unmistakable approach to theatre.

The Royal Shakespeare Company is incorporated under Royal Charter.

Registered Charity Number 212481

The RSC relies on the active involvement and the direct charitable support of our audience members for contributions towards our work. Members of our audience also assist by introducing us to companies, foundations and other organisations with which they have an involvement – and help us demonstrate that in return for either philanthropic or sponsorship support, we can deliver benefit to audiences, local communities, school groups and all those who are given enhanced access to our work through private sector support.

RSC PATRONS AND SHAKESPEARE'S CIRCLE

Personal contributions from RSC Patrons provide essential financial support for our artists, educationalists and their students, young writers and audience members that require special access services. For more information, please contact Sophie Lopez-Welsch on **01789 403470**.

CORPORATE PARTNERSHIPS

The RSC has a global reputation, undertaking more international touring each year than any other UK arts organisation. Our profile is high; our core values of artistic excellence and outstanding performance can be aligned with commercial values and objectives. Our extensive range of productions and outreach and education programmes help ensure that we identify the best opportunity to deliver your particular business objectives. A prestigious programme of corporate hospitality and membership packages is also available. For more information, please contact Victoria Okotie on **0207 845 0509**.

For detailed information about opportunities to support the work of the RSC, visit **www.rsc.org.uk/support**

This production of *Beauty and the Beast* was first performed by the Royal Shakespeare Company in the Royal Shakespeare Theatre, on 1 December 2003

The Family

Dorothy Atkinson	Marie Claire
John Bowler	Jean Louis
Julie Legrand	Helene
Gary Sefton	Phillipe
Darren Tunstall	Andre
Sophie Winkleman	Veronique
Miltos Yerolemou	Emile

Beast's Palace

Dorothy Atkinson	Beast's Maid
Julie Legrand	The Witch
Adam Levy	Beast
Gary Sefton	Beast's Man
John Bowler	Wardrobe
Darren Tunstall	Wardrobe
Sophie Winkleman	Vanity Table
Miltos Yerolemou	Screen

Chorus

Phillip Aiden
Julie Barnes
Lee Boggess
Margie Chadwick
Sergio Covino
Nicola Filshie
David Lucas
Barry McNeill
Lucy Potter

Directed by	**Laurence Boswell**
Set designed by	**Jeremy Herbert**
Costumes designed by	**Kandis Cook**
Choreography by	**Stuart Hopps**
Lighting designed by	**Adam Silverman**
Music by	**Mick Sands**
Sound by	**Mic Pool**
Movement by	**Gary Sefton and Darren Tunstall**
Music Director	**John Woolf**
Casting Directors	**John Cannon and Hannah Miller**
Assistant Director	**Frances Moore**
Assistant Choreographer/Dance Captain	**Heather Habens**
Production Manager	**David Parker**
Costume Supervisor	**Anna Watkins**
Company voice work by	**Lyn Darnley and Charmian Hoare**
Company Manager	**Jondon**
Stage Manager	**Laura Deards**
Deputy Stage Manager	**Clare Fisher**
Assistant Stage Manager	**Alice Irving**

CHARACTERS

Family

JEAN LOUIS, *a wealthy merchant*
HELENE, *his wife*
ANDRE, *eldest son*
PHILLIPE, *second son*
EMILE, *youngest son*
VERONIQUE, *eldest daughter*
MARIE CLARE, *second daughter*
BEAUTY, *youngest daughter*

Palace

BEAST, PRINCE
BEAST'S MAN (Phillipe)
BEAST'S MAID (Marie Clare)
THE WITCH (Helene)

Furniture in Beauty's room:
WARDROBE (Jean Louis and Andre)
VANITY TABLE (Veronique)
SCREEN (Emile)

Chorus

SERVANTS *in Paris*
LIVESTOCK *on the farm*
FATHER'S HORSE
STAGE SERVANTS
BEAST'S HORSE
PALACE CHORUS
ROOM OF MIRRORS
KING OF MIRRORS

ACT ONE

Scene One: Paris

CHORUS *enter, enigmatic, sardonic. Reveal the family of* JEAN LOUIS.

HELENE. Long ago. In a city far away. There lived a merchant.

JEAN LOUIS. Who was so successful in all his business speculations that he grew enormously rich!

HELENE. Which was handy because he had six children!

BOYS. Three boys!

GIRLS. Three girls!

JEAN LOUIS. And a staff of twenty-seven!!

HELENE. The merchant's eldest son . . .

ANDRE. Was incredibly intelligent! (ANDRE *falls over.*)

KIDS. Ha! Ha! Ha!

SERVANTS *help him up.*

HELENE. He spent hours in the library with his head in books.

JEAN LOUIS. His latest obsession being astrology!

KIDS. Astronomy.

ANDRE. Papa!

JEAN LOUIS. Isn't that what I just said!

KIDS. No!

HELENE *invites* ANDRE *to continue.*

ANDRE. There are millions of suns in the universe, so the chance of there being other forms of life out there is statisti . . .

JEAN LOUIS. That's enough now.

HELENE. Sit down, Andre. There's a good boy.

ANDRE. But Maman, I don't want to sit down. I have yet to speak of the constellation of . . .

JEAN LOUIS. Don't, disobey your mother!

ANDRE *yields and prepares to sit.*

HELENE. Merci, Andre.

ANDRE. C'est rien maman. (ANDRE *falls over.* SERVANTS *assist.*)

KIDS. Ha! Ha! Ha!

JEAN LOUIS. Mes enfants!

HELENE. The merchant's second son.

PHILLIPE *leaps onto chair.*

PHILLIPE. Papa! (*Pulls ball from his coat.*)

HELENE. Loved all kinds of sport!

PHILLIPE *throws ball to his* DAD.

He spent his days playing football, tennis and . . .

PHILLIPE. Rugby!

PHILLIPE *runs, evading servants and kids.* JEAN LOUIS *takes and returns a pass.*

HELENE. Sit down now! That's enough!

He scores a try.

ALL. La triomphe!

HELENE. His clothes were always untidy and his knees were constantly grazed.

PHILLIPE. Maman!

PHILLIPE *does cartwheels and somersaults. Kids clap and do a parody.*

HELENE. Sit down now. There's a good boy.

PHILLIPE. But Maman, I don't want to sit down.

JEAN LOUIS. Don't disobey your mother!

PHILLIPE *sits.*

HELENE. Merci, Phillipe.

PHILLIPE. C'est rien maman. (*Sits, then up abruptly with tennis racket.*)

Papa!?

HELENE. Just sit still!

JEAN LOUIS *gestures to* PHILLIPE *to calm down.*

JEAN LOUIS. The merchant's youngest son . . .

EMILE. Ma ma mère!

Waves to MUM. *She waves back.*

HELENE. Mon petit chou!

EMILE *on his* MUM*'s lap, lots of kisses.*

JEAN LOUIS. Was dreadfully indulged by his mother.

HELENE. Mama bought Meelie big machine for makey icey cream!

EMILE. But I want play Phillish!

HELENE. Then you can play with Phillish!!

KIDS. Urgh!!

EMILE *has sword fight with* PHILLIPE. DAD *tries to get the sword.*

JEAN LOUIS. Give me that!

EMILE. My sword, papa!

Keeps the sword away from DAD.

Maman?

HELENE. You keep it, darling.

KIDS. Uhh?

HELENE. But do sit down now, there's a good boy!

EMILE *puts sword in coat.*

EMILE. Meelie. Don't want, sit down.

JEAN LOUIS. Down!!

EMILE *sits down very fast.*

HELENE. Merci, Emile.

EMILE. C'est rien maman.

EMILE *up, pulls faces behind* JEAN LOUIS*'s back.* MUM *smiles and wags a warning finger.* KIDS *try to warn* JEAN LOUIS *who has seen nothing.*

KIDS. Papa!

EMILE *gets back into his place.*

JEAN LOUIS. What's going on?

HELENE. Nothing dear!

KIDS. Nothing much!

HELENE. The Merchant loved his sons.

BOYS. Papa!

JEAN LOUIS. Mes enfants!

HELENE. But his pride and joy were his daughters . . .

JEAN LOUIS. The eldest girl was . . . utterly . . . (*He can't find the exact word.*)

BOYS. Ugly!

VERONIQUE. Charming and graceful!

JEAN LOUIS. She was especially . . .

BOYS. Spiteful!

VERONIQUE. Gifted as a cellist!

JEAN LOUIS. At school she always . . .

BOYS. Cheated in exams!

VERONIQUE. Came top of her class!

JEAN LOUIS. She was academically brilliant . . .

BOYS. She copied Andre's homework.

VERONIQUE. With no apparent effort!

BOYS. She copied Andre's homework.

JEAN LOUIS. Her school report was full of . . .

BOYS. Lies!

VERONIQUE. Embarrassing praise!

JEAN LOUIS. She was fluent in . . .

BOYS. Lies!!

VERONIQUE. Latin, Greek and Italian!

JEAN LOUIS. Her essays were adorned with . . .

BOYS. Lies.

VERONIQUE *turns.*

Argh!!

VERONIQUE *mashes* BOYS. PARENTS *miss it, reading report.*

VERONIQUE. Her essays were adorned with, gold star, admiration!

JEAN LOUIS. You are so very clever Veronique!

VERONIQUE. And?

Painful pause.

JEAN LOUIS. What?

HELENE. Beautiful?

BOYS. Not!!

JEAN LOUIS. Yes. Yes, yes of course.

HELENE. Merci, Veronique. (HELENE *invites* VERONIQUE *to sit.*)

VERONIQUE. C'est rien mamam. (VERONIQUE *sits down, very sad.*)

BOYS. Ha! Ha! Ha!

JEAN LOUIS. I don't know what's . . . What did I say?

HELENE. You wouldn't understand.

JEAN LOUIS. What!?

HELENE. The Merchant's second daughter . . .

JEAN LOUIS. Was very, very . . .

BOYS. Stupid!

MARIE CLARE. Different to her big sister.

JEAN LOUIS. She was really, really . . .

BOYS. Thick!

MARIE CLARE. Less interested in her studies.

JEAN LOUIS. She was exceptionally . . .

BOYS. Boring!

MARIE CLARE. Pretty and attractive . . .

JEAN LOUIS. Her mind was full of . . .

BOYS. Sawdust!

MARIE CLARE. Wedding dresses and pink ponies . . .

JEAN LOUIS. And her heart was full of . . .

BOYS. Poison!

MARIE CLARE. Romantic heroes and high-status husbands.

JEAN LOUIS. The twin passions of her life . . .

BOYS. Vanity and pride!

MARIE CLARE. Were fashion and cosmetics!

BOYS. Vanity and pride!

JEAN LOUIS. Her greatest talent was . . .

BOYS. Vanity and pride!

MARIE CLARE. Dancing!

Dance. Applause. MARIE CLARE *creates cloud of scent,* BOYS *choke.*

BOYS. Ergh!!

HELENE. Merci, Marie Clare.

MARIE CLARE. C'est rien maman.

HELENE. The eldest girls were either the best of friends . . .

VERONIQUE. Promise to be my best, best friend until you die.

MARIE CLARE. On s'embrace.

VERONIQUE. Mais oui, d'accord.

HELENE. Or the worst of enemies.

VERONIQUE *is holding a broken cello bow.*

VERONIQUE. I'm gonna rip out her liver!!

ANDRE. Maman!

MAIDS *arrive at speed to sort out the disturbance.*

VERONIQUE. And set fire to her hair!

EMILE. Help!

More STAFF *arrive to stop the fight, looking worried.*

MARIE CLARE. Over here, spotty, swotty, ugly girl!

The SISTERS *spy each other and square up to fight.*

VERONIQUE. Say ya prayers. Bun head!

BOYS. FIGHT! FIGHT! FIGHT! FIGHT! FIGHT!

Music. GIRLS *fight.* BOYS *join in. All try to stop it. All tangled. Baby cries. Slow motion. Baby is doll.* BEAUTY *animates doll which represents herself as a baby.*

HELENE. If the eldest girls could never agree on anything, for very long, there was one thing which united them . . .

PHILIPPE *and* EMILE. Always!

ANDRE. Always and forever!

HELENE. And that was the birth of our sixth child!

KIDS. Uuh!

Baby BEAUTY *pops out of the morass of bodies.*

CHORUS. Aah!!

JEAN LOUIS. Even as a tiny baby she was so wise and so confident . . .

HELENE. She seemed, almost, to know us all, already.

JEAN LOUIS. We couldn't find a name for her at first and then . . .

BEAUTY. Que . . . le monde . . . est . . . beau.

JEAN LOUIS. Her very first words . . .

BEAUTY. Que . . . le monde . . . est . . . beau.

HELENE. How . . . beautiful . . . is this world . . .

JEAN LOUIS. What a bizarre thing to say!

HELENE. Perhaps, we should call her . . . Beauty.

JEAN LOUIS. Splendid idea!!

ANDRE. Parents!!

BOYS. Think of the implications!

ANDRE *points to the elder sisters, who are furious.*

VERONIQUE. I've looked this up in a very large book Papa and 'Beauty' is not a proper name!

MARIE CLARE. She should be called . . . crying, blob!

VERONIQUE. Crying, smelly, vomiting, blob! From Hell!

MARIE CLARE. Exactly!

VERONIQUE. Couldn't we send her back now, papa?

MARIE CLARE. Right!!

VERONIQUE. Or have her adopted?

BEAUTY. Flying Beauty!!!

PHILLIPE *throws doll high into the air,* ANDRE *catches.*

HELENE. The boys soon fell in love with their little sister . . .

BEAUTY *offers doll to elder sisters, they walk away.*

VERONIQUE *and* MARIE CLARE. Don't want to play with you. Blob!!

HELENE. But the eldest girls could never quite forgive Beauty for coming into the world.

BEAUTY. Flying Baddies!!!

BEAUTY *throws doll.* EMILE *catches and runs from imaginary enemies.*

HELENE. Beauty took it all in her stride. In fact she was so self-contained and so modest that I sometimes found it hard to believe that she was actually one of ours.

JEAN LOUIS. Shark attack!

BOYS *and* DAD *rush down stage and animate model ships.*

HELENE. The boys worshipped their father. They listened in wonder to his tales of dangerous and distant lands where he traded spices, silks and precious stones.

GIRLS *grab* JEAN LOUIS.

JEAN LOUIS. The eldest girls enjoyed a glamorous and glittering lifestyle.

During this the GIRLS *fan themselves and dance about* PARENTS.

Regularly attending gala evenings at the opera, the ballet and the theatre.

JEAN LOUIS *invites them to speak.*

VERONIQUE. Last night, in our box at the ballet, I was offered a chocolate by the youngest daughter of the Countess du Camembert, who is third reserve, lady in waiting, to her majesty!!!

MARIE CLARE. At the stage door of the Theatre Royal last week the King's tennis coach kissed me full on the lips. Then put his hand on my . . .

VERONIQUE *stops* MARIE CLARE *finishing.* JEAN LOUIS *concerned.*

JEAN LOUIS. What?

HELENE. Girls, papa has arranged for you to meet the very eligible sons of Monsieur Fournier and Monsieur Barrault!

VERONIQUE. Barrault! The vinegar merchant?!?!

MARIE CLARE. Fournier! The horse meat millionaire!?!?

VERONIQUE. Papa, I'll marry a Count!

MARIE CLARE. Papa, I'll marry a Prince!

JEAN LOUIS. But not the son of a merchant!!

MARIE CLARE. No.

VERONIQUE. Never.

MARIE CLARE. No.

VERONIQUE. Never.

BOTH. No! No! No!

HELENE. The family lived in a beautiful and expensive house in the fashionable and exclusive heart of . . .

ALL. PARIS!!!

JEAN LOUIS. The house had been especially designed for the Merchant. It was the envy of all his business partners.

HELENE. It had twelve bedrooms.

JEAN LOUIS. A staff of thirty six!

CHORUS *change hats and bow to audience.*

HELENE. A ballroom, a stable, extensive servants' quarters . . .

MARIE CLARE. And a live-in ballet master!!! (*Much strange subtext.*)

HELENE. But despite its size . . .

JEAN LOUIS. Twelve bedrooms, over four floors, with a staff of forty five!

STAFF *change hats and bow to audience.*

HELENE. The eldest girls were always complaining.

VERONIQUE. I need a library of my own now, papa.

HELENE. But despite the little frustrations and difficulties . . .

MARIE CLARE. We've only got three fountains?!

HELENE. The family were happy!

JEAN LOUIS *embraces* HELENE, *at his wit's end.*

In their own way!

JEAN LOUIS *hugging* HELENE *close.*

JEAN LOUIS. The years ran like water through our fingers.

HELENE *hugs* JEAN LOUIS *hard.*

HELENE. And the children grew up so quickly!

JEAN LOUIS*'s head buried in wife.*

Everyday seemed to be somebody's birthday!

Music. SERVANTS *come forward with, food, party hats, cake.*

JEAN LOUIS. The 7th of May!

HELENE. Beauty's fifth birthday!

Blind man's bluff. HELENE *blindfolded. All sing,* STAFF *harmonising.*

Birthday Song.

C'est à ton tour,
Ma chère amie,
De nous laisser, parler d'amour.
C'est à ton tour,
Ma chère amie,
De nous laisser, parler d'amour.

BEAUTY. The 7th of May. The day my mother died.

HELENE *takes her blindfold off and exits during* BEAUTY*'s song.*

Song of Lament.

O maman, ma chère maman,
Tu m'as quitté, tu es partie,
Tu ne viens pas quand je . . .

BEAUTY *can't complete the song.*

My mother loved me, she held me, she kissed me and then she died.

JEAN LOUIS *grabs boats. Throws them away, violently.*

ANDRE. The merchant threw himself into his work.

KIDS. Papa!

ANDRE. He spent recklessly!

KIDS. Papa!!

ANDRE. Invested foolishly!!

KIDS. Stop it!!!

ANDRE. He made dubious deals with dishonest partners.

Kids and staff gather in huddle to view an unfolding disaster.

KIDS. Look!!!

ANDRE. What??

JEAN LOUIS. No!!

ANDRE. Their beautiful house . . .

VERONIQUE. School reports!

MARIE CLARE. Ballet slippers!

EMILE. Toys!

ANDRE. Burnt down to the ground.

House flies out. KIDS *try to stop it leaving.*

PHILLIPE. Then the merchant's business collapsed.

KIDS. Why!?

Group reveal JEAN LOUIS *drunk, filling another champagne flute.*

PHILLIPE. Storms sunk his ships . . .

KIDS. No!

JEAN LOUIS *drinking from the bottle now, finishing the dregs.*

PHILLIPE. Dishonest partners ran away taking all that was left of the merchant's fortune . . .

JEAN LOUIS *hurls bottle.* FAMILY *come downstage centre in a long line.*

KIDS. From wealth and comfort the family sank into poverty!

JEAN LOUIS *drops like a stone.*

Staff unpaid.

Difficult pause.

BEAUTY. There's no money . . . to pay you . . . I'm sorry.

Valet gives ANDRE *deeds.* STAFF *leave. Waving goodbye.*

KIDS. Au revoir.

ANDRE. All that was left of the merchant's empire was . . .

VERONIQUE. A derelict, farmhouse . . .

PHILLIPE. And, assorted, livestock . . .

MARIE CLARE. What does that say?

EMILE. IN . . . THE . . . COUNTRY!

ANDRE. The eldest girls were horrified at the prospect of living in such an isolated spot, horrified at the prospect of . . .

MARIE CLARE. Slugs!

VERONIQUE. Snakes!

MARIE CLARE. Provincial people!!!

VERONIQUE. Papa, this rural folly is simply out of the question. Our dear, dear friends at court would be simply suicidal at the prospect, you go if you must, Marie Clare and myself are staying put.

MARIE CLARE. What she said.

EMILE. What's wrong with papa?

MARIE CLARE. He's sulking!

BEAUTY. He's grieving!

MARIE CLARE. Feeling sorry for himself.

BEAUTY. His heart's broken!

BOYS. Papa!!

No response from JEAN LOUIS, KIDS *getting very worried.*

EMILE. There's no one to look after us.

VERONIQUE. Look, he made some stupid business decisions and now he's bankrupt he thinks he can just bury his head in the sand, well it's not good enough, because let's face it, who's actually going to suffer for all this at the end of the day?

ANDRE. Veronique!!!

VERONIQUE. Exactly!!! And this is such a bad time for me! Why doesn't papa just get up and do something, the stupid, selfish . . . Urh. Get up and find me a husband! I need a father not a failure!

Furious and dangerous, VERONIQUE *breaks down and sobs bitterly.*

ANDRE. What's this?

ANDRE *takes a very sodden letter from the sobbing* VERONIQUE.

VERONIQUE. From, my, best, best friend.

ANDRE *reads,* VERONIQUE *sobs throughout.*

ANDRE. Dearest V, so sorry to hear about the awful disasters which have assailed you of late, but I'm afraid I just can't help. I'm so busy right now what with end-of-year exams, skiing and tennis, I really don't have a second. Mentioned your troubles to mama, she said they were a judgment from God on your vanity, envy, spite and pride! Seems a bit harsh, but worth thinking about, eh? Enjoy the country V, Yours . . . Camembert.

PHILLIPE. Your best friend!

VERONIQUE *springs out of her hell of despair.*

VERONIQUE. I'll rip you in half! Bully boy! (VERONIQUE *sobs backs down.*)

BEAUTY (*sings*).

Song Of Lament.

O maman, ma chère maman,
Tu m'as quitté, tu es partie,
Tu ne viens pas quand je pleurs,
Je cherche en vain mon âme soeur.
O maman ma chère maman,
Il n'y a personne pour me recomforter.

KIDS *repeat song, hanging clothes and wigs on hangers, descended from the flies.* JEAN LOUIS *hasn't moved.* KIDS *tense.* JEAN LOUIS *drags himself up.*

JEAN LOUIS. Goodbye, Paris. Goodbye, old life. Goodbye . . .

Another verse, instrumental. JEAN LOUIS *hangs his stuff on the hanger. Clothes fly out, swing flies in. Enter* CHORUS. KIDS *mount swing.*

Let's go!

JEAN LOUIS *chucks reins,* CHORUS *propel the swing, off they go. Singing.*

To the Country.

Les mains qui bougent et le dos pliant
Ils font du bon travail.
Et la bonne terre prend toutes les plantes,
Qui portent fruits sans faille.
Tra, la la la, tra la la la la.

Le bon travail fait du succès,
Je compte gagner ma croûte.
Allons-y, mes vieux fermiers.

C'est la bonne vie, sans doute.
Tra, la la la, tra la la la la.
Charrue, semence, blé moissonné.
Les vaches dans la campagne.
Chèvre, coq, canard, poulets,
Les fruits de la besogne.

Scene Two: The Country

CHORUS *stop swing, create country.* FAMILY *disembark.*

LOUIS. Whoa!

VERONIQUE. What's that bleak expanse of mud and grass?

BEAUTY. The country.

MARIE CLARE. And that big, tall, green thing?

BEAUTY. Is a tree!

VERONIQUE. And the pile of old stones?

PHILLIPE. Our new home!

MARIE CLARE. Tell us it's not true!

VERONIQUE. We can't live here, papa!

JEAN LOUIS. It's all we have left.

PHILLIPE. If we want shelter we must repair that cottage, if we want to eat we must plant seeds in the earth, we must pull fish from the river and draw water from the well.

CHORUS *become animals.* VERONIQUE *screams. Something behind her.*

VERONIQUE. Ugh!!

MARIE CLARE. What's that??

PHILLIPE. Dinner!!

Music. Animsal hunt. Then FAMILY *work. Make a new home. Sleep.*

BEAUTY. It was hard! Those first months! Our soft city hands soon got blistered and cracked, you see, none of us had ever done any kind of physical work before! In Paris we'd lived in a kind of dream, a dream that rested on the efforts of others. We had servants, to dress us, to put food in our mouths, to tidy up our mess, so, it wasn't easy, digging fields all day and going to sleep exhausted and hungry and getting up at five in the morning to shovel horse dung and clean out pigs.

PHILLIPE. Wakey, wakey! (*Banging a triangle.*) Rise and shine!

Music. FAMILY *and* ANIMALS *don Christmas hats, sit round a table.*

BEAUTY. By the time Christmas day arrived, we'd made life bearable.

JEAN LOUIS *lifts the lid on a big Christmas turkey.*

ALL. Dinner!

Music. FAMILY *devour a big Christmas dinner, very fast.*

Aaahh!

PHILLIPE *making speech with bottle of home-made wine.*

PHILLIPE. We've picked enough grapes this year to make half a dozen bottles of our own wine. Happy Christmas!! (*Swigs wine, it's really rough.*) That's good. Very, very good!!

ANDRE *seizes the bottle.*

ANDRE. I've repaired a stone wall, tickled three trout and I haven't fallen over once, in five months. Happy Christmas. Everyone. (*Takes a swig. Just about hides his total disgust.*) Um. Nice!

EMILE *seizes bottle.*

EMILE. This year I skinned a rabbit and stole some honey from a bee's house. Cheers! (EMILE *swigs the home-made wine, spits it out immediately.*) Urgh. Disgusting!!

VERONIQUE *and* MARIE CLARE *laugh, sneer and gloat.* ROOSTER *enters with letter in beak.*

MARIE CLARE. What's that?

EMILE *takes letter from the rooster's beak.*

EMILE. A . . . letter . . . for . . . Papa!?

FATHER *nervously breaks the seal and reads. Tense silence.*

JEAN LOUIS. Oh, dear!

ANDRE. Bad news?!!

JEAN LOUIS. One of my ships, which had been feared lost, is found!

EMILE. Papa!!

JEAN LOUIS. 'The *Star of the Morning Sky* is standing in the port of Marseilles, with a cargo, of pearls.'

MARIE CLARE. How much is that worth?

JEAN LOUIS. Millions . . .

Pause.

MARIE CLARE. Thank God!

VERONIQUE. The end of poverty!

ANDRE. How far is Marseilles?

VERONIQUE. Better get going now!

MARIE CLARE. Will you bring us back presents?

JEAN LOUIS. Yes, of course.

PHILLIPE. But we need you in the fields.

JEAN LOUIS. I'll be back.

VERONIQUE. We're going back to the Paris!

JEAN LOUIS. Right!

PHILLIPE. We're staying in the country!

JEAN LOUIS. Right!

VERONIQUE. First nights at the ballet.

JEAN LOUIS. Posh frocks and tiaras.

EMILE. We'll need a bull for the cows!

JEAN LOUIS. I'll get two!

ANDRE. Papa, it's really important for you to be very clear at this point.

MARIE CLARE. Posh nosh with posh chaps!

JEAN LOUIS. Right!!

PHILLIPE. We need a wine press!

JEAN LOUIS. Yes!

MARIE CLARE. Rivers of perfume . . .

JEAN LOUIS. Flowing and flooding!

EMILE. A machine for making ice cream!

JEAN LOUIS. It's coming, it's coming!

ANDRE. Papa, you've set up an impossible situation . . .

JEAN LOUIS. You can all have everything, everything your little hearts desire!

ANDRE. It's not possible to say yes, to both parties, because what they each want is mutually exclusive and although it might make you feel good, saying yes to everybody all the time, it's an unsustainable position and when you finally make a decision on this, one party is going to feel really disappointed. And hurt!

JEAN LOUIS. Andre! You're absolutely right.

VERONIQUE. So, we're going back to Paris!

JEAN LOUIS. Yes!!

PHILLIPE. We're staying on the farm!

JEAN LOUIS. Right!!

ANDRE. I give up I totally just give up . . . (ANDRE *falls over.*)

MARIE CLARE *and* VERONIQUE. Ha! Ha! Ha!

VERONIQUE. We've climbed out of the pit of poverty and fallen back into . . .

MARIE CLARE *and* VERONIQUE. The lap of luxury!

MARIE CLARE. Why's . . . she . . so quiet?

VERONIQUE. Just another attention-grabbing strategy.

JEAN LOUIS. Beauty! What can I bring you?

BEAUTY. Just, come home safely!

MARIE CLARE. What a prig!

BEAUTY. Beware of making promises you can't keep!

JEAN LOUIS. Let me buy you a present!

BEAUTY. Who knows what will happen in Marseilles?

JEAN LOUIS. One gift won't break us.

MARIE CLARE. What's she up to?

BEAUTY. There is something, papa.

VERONIQUE. Here, it comes.

The music of the rose underscores this section.

BEAUTY. Bring me, a rose! A wild, red, rose! (*Pause.*)

It will cost you little. (*Pause.*)

And it can be my dowry!

JEAN LOUIS *and* BEAUTY *stare at each other.*

VERONIQUE. It's sad she feels compelled to walk this crooked path.

MARIE CLARE. What crooked path?

VERONIQUE. She's trying to make herself look virtuous with her humble request.

MARIE CLARE. I'd like to rip out her windpipe and dance in her lungs.

ANDRE. Listen to what they're saying, papa . . .

VERONIQUE. We'll cut out her eyes and eat them them off a spit!

ANDRE. You must deal with this.

JEAN LOUIS. Girls! Please! Less of your high spirits.

ANDRE. Why do I bother? (ANDRE *falls over again.*)

JEAN LOUIS. Beauty. It's too soon for you to be thinking of marriage! You'll be required to keep your father company for many years yet to come.

BEAUTY. Soon, I will leave here and make my own life.

JEAN LOUIS. I forbid you to think such thoughts! D'you hear?!

BEAUTY *turns away. No reply.*

Beauty?

Pause.

MARIE CLARE. What's going on?

VERONIQUE. Saddle up, papa!

JEAN LOUIS. Right. Children. Fetch me my horse!

Enter HELENE, *full-length riding coat. Carrying horse's head and riding crop.* CHORUS *behind her creating body of the merchant's horse.*

Le cheval de mon père,
Le cheval de mon père,
Le cheval de mon père,
Va bien, il va bien.

Le cheval de mon père,
Le cheval de mon père,
Le cheval de mon père,
Se n'arrête rien.

A Encore la richesse,
Tra la la la la.

B Va tiens la tristesse,
Tra la la la la.

A Vive la cité, le prospérité!

B Ah! Mais non! C'est dans la campagne!

A Vive la cité, pour vivre en liberté!

B Ah! Mais non! C'est dans la campagne!

Dance tells the story of the thrills and terror of a wild journey. A galloping, stamping dance full of excitement, expectation and hope. Dance ends abruptly. Music changes. HORSE *transforms into ship. Masts. Sails. Sailors climbing ropes. The noise of a port fills the air.* JEAN LOUIS *stands on the prow, proud and happy, his arms full of money, he is staring out to sea, happy at last.*

ALL. The Star of the Morning Sky!!

Scene Three: Father's Journey

HELENE *removes horse's head. She is narrator, horse and ghost.*

HELENE. The ship had arrived in port as the letter had promised, but the merchant's dishonest partners had repossessed it and sold it off cheaply, for a quick profit, and though the merchant took his partners to law to reclaim what was rightfully his and though he proved his case, the legal proceedings took nine months and the cost of the litigation, left the merchant, with nothing!

Music. Ship dissolves. JEAN LOUIS *lowered to the ground.*

HELENE. His fortune had escaped him. To add to his disappointment.

JEAN LOUIS. Come on old nag.

HELENE. As he began his journey home.

Music. CHORUS *create snow storm.*

A snow storm blew up!!!

JEAN LOUIS *and* HORSE *stand still, overwhelmed.*

Despite the icy winds and the blasting snow, the merchant was determined to get home to his children.

JEAN LOUIS. Come on girl!!

They trudge forward very slowly. Stop.

HELENE. He made a mighty vow in the core of his heart . . .

Musical flourish, struggle against elements.

And pushed on into the storm.

They struggle on. CHORUS *create forest.*

Then. Night fell.

HELENE *lights a match.*

They were deep in a freezing cold forest.

JEAN LOUIS. We're lost! (JEAN LOUIS, *consults map and compass. Gives up.)* Without, shelter, we'll freeze to death.

Scary wolf, owl, toad sounds. HORSE *hides behind* JEAN LOUIS *in terror.*

Or be ripped in pieces!

Music. Trudge a few steps. CHORUS *create an old hollow tree.*

JEAN LOUIS. What's that?

HELENE. An old, hollow, tree!

JEAN LOUIS. Let's get inside!

Music. JEAN LOUIS *drops* HORSE *and runs to tree. Lights an old candle end.*

There we are. That'll help. Come on, old girl, cuddle up.

HELENE *not sure about the cuddle.*

Tonight might be our last night on earth.

They hug and rub each other.

Whatever happens, stay awake!

Prays, in embrace with horse.

Oh, merciful lord. Protect my children. Help them to grow up strong and true. Help them to love you and all your works . . . look after them in this world and take them to heaven to live with you in bliss. Our father who art in heaven . . .

HELENE *and* JEAN LOUIS. Amen.

HELENE. Wearied with exhaustion and shaking with cold . . .

JEAN LOUIS. Stay awake!

HELENE. They drifted into sleep!

Owls and wolves. HELENE *blows out candle.* CHORUS *create dawn.*

Slowly the sun emerged from behind the mountains, dissolving the night and splashing the snow-whitened trees with the delicate gold and the soft pink of a brand new day.

HELENE. He thanked God for sparing his life.

JEAN LOUIS. Our father! Hail Mary! Amen! Come here. (*Gives* HORSE *hug.*) We've lived to fight another day!

HELENE. He gave his horse a crippling hug.

JEAN LOUIS *drops hug fast.*

JEAN LOUIS. But – where's the path?

HELENE. Snow had completely carpeted the forest floor!

JEAN LOUIS. We'll head due north!

Trying to travel, HORSE *slips on the ice.*

HELENE. Sheets of ice hid beneath the snow.

Slips. JEAN LOUIS *picks her up, walks.* JEAN LOUIS *drops* HORSE *and falls to the ground, exhausted.*

They struggled on, not knowing where they were going . . . And then, at the point of complete despair, when they had given up all hope, they saw . . .

JEAN LOUIS. A shimmering, translucent Palace . . .

HELENE. Visible and invisible all at once!

Wild sitar music.

A path of pearls led to the palace, on either side were . . .

JEAN LOUIS. Orange trees . . .

HELENE. Bursting with blossom and heavy with fruit . . .

JEAN LOUIS. Blossom and fruit? . . .

HELENE. Said the merchant, who was confused . . .

JEAN LOUIS. I'm confused!

HELENE. 'Who cares,' thought the horse, who wasn't confused but delighted!

JEAN LOUIS. I'm sorry but how can there be both blossom and fruit?And where's that carpet of snow?

HELENE. Before he could conclude his important contemplations.

Music. A knotted rope descends from the flies.

A stairway appeared!

The banisters were made of ivory and the steps were solid gold.

JEAN LOUIS *climbs the rope ladder up into the air,* CHORUS *assist.*

Up, he climbed. Higher and higher. Higher and higher. Soon, he was above the clouds. The forest stretched out beneath him like a frozen lake and when he reached the top, he stopped and screamed . . .

JEAN LOUIS. I'm standing, on the roof, of the world!

HELENE. He saw a lapis lazuli door. With a handle of tears. He opened the door. Stepped inside and . . .

JEAN LOUIS. AHH!

JEAN LOUIS *down.* CHORUS *exit. Lies motionless.* HORSE *enters palace. Sniffs* JEAN LOUIS, *lies next to him wondering what will happen. Enter Palace* CHORUS *with lighted candelabra.*

The merchant woke to find himself in a huge hall at the heart of the Palace.

Sniffing the air, the merchant becomes animated again.

JEAN LOUIS. What's that smell??

HELENE. The scent of jasmine filled the air.

JEAN LOUIS. Oh, my giddy aunt!

HELENE. He was overwhelmed by the magnificence of the architecture.

JEAN LOUIS. Will ya cop a look at that!

JEAN LOUIS *puts shades on and plays with light.*

HELENE. And astonished at the sunlight, streaming and flooding through the stained-glass windows.

JEAN LOUIS. Ooo!!

HELENE. His stomach rumbled.

JEAN LOUIS. Pardon me.

HELENE. He hadn't eaten for two days.

JEAN LOUIS. I'm starving!

HELENE. The instant hunger gripped his stomach . . .

CHORUS *offer dishes containing many kinds of food.*

JEAN LOUIS. Meat! Cake! Snails!

HELENE. Food filled the room.

Music. A frenzy of eating and drinking.

JEAN LOUIS. Now. I must find my host and thank him for this fabulous feast.

JEAN LOUIS *explores the palace.* CHORUS *suggest the rooms.*

HELENE. As he scuttled down empty corridors.

JEAN LOUIS. Thank you.

HELENE. He was concerned.

JEAN LOUIS. Thank you. (*Whispered.*)

HELENE. 'Cause he couldn't spot a living soul.

JEAN LOUIS. Thank you.

HELENE. Couldn't even spy a servant!

JEAN LOUIS. Thank you.

HELENE. Each room was utterly empty.

JEAN LOUIS. Thank you.

HELENE. One was the size of a football field.

JEAN LOUIS. Thank you.

HELENE. On the ceiling suns shone, moons spun, and eagles soared. On the walls tapestries teemed with tremulous life, kingfishers dived into turbulent rivers and swirling clouds of butterflies flapped tiny embroidered wings. On the floor was a carpet of dreams, rippling with a million colours and wet with as many tears. Just as the merchant was wondering what such a carpet would look like in a delicate shade of softest pink . . .

CHORUS *swing candelabra down to the carpet.*

JEAN LOUIS. Carpet! Turned! Pink!

HELENE. The merchant had suffered many years of grief and bitter disappointment, he'd lost a home, a business and a wife . . .

JEAN LOUIS. Pink, pink, pinkety, pink . . .

HELENE. Yet here, in the intense magic of the palace, his pain began to melt like a snowball in a pan of boiling water . . .

JEAN LOUIS. Tcha, tcha. Tcha, cha, char!!

HELENE. Images of glory were reborn in his brain.

JEAN LOUIS. Hoole, oola, oo, lapa, dapa, dar.

HELENE. He was hurling unhappiness out of his heart.

JEAN LOUIS. Shalloo-shalla, Shallapa dapa, dar.

HELENE. Shaking sweet sadness out of his soul!

JEAN LOUIS. Ha! Ha! Ha! Ha! Ha! Ha! Ha! Even Veronique and Marie Clare would be happy to live here! (JEAN LOUIS *blows raspberry, does the twist.*)

HELENE. He was . . . alive! He was . . . happy! He was . . . free!

JEAN LOUIS. Finders, keepers! Losers, weepers!

CHORUS *blow out candles.*

Tak'a tak'a tak'a tak'a tak!

HELENE. The merchant began to run about the Palace, making an inventory of all its precious treasures . . .

JEAN LOUIS. Shalak a laca a laca a lak a lak.

HELENE. Treasures, he now believed belonged to him!!!

JEAN LOUIS. Galopa, lopa: lopa, lap.

HELENE. Lost in his dreams of wealth and power, he galloped into the Gardens of The Palace.

JEAN LOUIS *admires Palace gardens.*

JEAN LOUIS. What odiferous odours, have these, opal, orchids!!!

HELENE. He was very far gone.

JEAN LOUIS. You sensuous, sexy, statues!

HELENE. He felt like a man again!

JEAN LOUIS. What breathtaking topiary!!!

HELENE. Ready to resume his position . . .

JEAN LOUIS. A cup of cottage cheese, Count??!!

HELENE. At the pinnacle of prosperous . . .

JEAN LOUIS. A hunk of hamon, your Highness? . . .

HELENE. And fashionable . . .

JEAN LOUIS. A piece of pineapple, Prince?

HELENE. Parisian society!

JEAN LOUIS. Shillip, shillip: shillip, shalp, shlop! Ha! Ha!

I love this place, this, palace, which, is, mine, mine, mine!!! Men, am, a, na. Na, na, na-nana! Men, am, a, na, Na, na, na-na. Men, am, a, na, Na, na, na-nana, na-nana, na, na, na, na, nananoo!

Music. JEAN LOUIS *does a little dance. Extremely relaxed and very silly.*

Sister butterfly! Come, leave off tapestry duty sister. Come, float about mine ears, sweet wing. Let me feel hot breath on me neck. (*He is kissed on the neck.*) Oo, sweet. Umn. Kisses? Naughty, sister! (JEAN LOUIS *convulses as he is licked by butterfly.*) And licks. Urgh. I can't resist. I shall lose my wits to your wicked, long licks. Ah. Ooh. Ooh. Ooh. Yes Yes. Oo. Urr. Us. Us. Ooo. Oooo.

A pantomime of erotic flirtation, noises and play. Abrupt change.

Brother sun! Hide your blushes. In the west! Oh, yes, I'm talking to you! Come on! Move it, matey! Let's go. Come on. Sun down in the west. You know the score. Come on. Chop, chop. Chop, chop. Chop, chop. (*Stops, falls and sobs.*)

HELENE. A path of pearls and a handle of tears . . .

JEAN LOUIS. I thought I'd die in poverty, a failure in my children's eyes.

HELENE. And then he saw . . . THE ROSE BUSH!!!

HELENE *holds up rose.* JEAN LOUIS *goes to rose, it dances away.* HELENE *and* JEAN LOUIS *dance.* CHORUS *create trap. Exit* HELENE. *Exit* CHORUS. JEAN LOUIS *takes scissors and cuts rose. Blood spurts. Roar of* BEAST. *Enter* BEAST *and* CHORUS *and* BEAST'S MAN. JEAN LOUIS *is caught by* CHORUS, *tethered upside down on rope.* BEAST *roars.*

BEAST'S MAN. Who, gave you, permission, steal, master's, rose!?!

JEAN LOUIS. I . . . I . . . I . . . Help! Help!

BEAST'S MAN. Nothing, can . . . h . . . h . . . help you, now.

BEAST. INGRATITUDE.

JEAN LOUIS. What?

BEAST'S MAN. You t, t, tasted, pleasure, now, s . . . s . . . steal, master's, rose!

JEAN LOUIS. But I didn't, know it belonged to . . .

BEAST. EXCUSES.

BEAST'S MAN. N, n, no excuses.

JEAN LOUIS. You, see I'm just . . .

BEAST. PUNISH.

BEAST'S MAN. Master, will, punish. You.

JEAN LOUIS. Mercy. Mighty. Lord!

BEAST. FLATTERY!

BEAST'S MAN. Not Lord. Beast. Master, hates, flat, flat, flattery!

JEAN LOUIS. Beast, in the name of justice and mercy and truth, I beg you, let me speak. Don't condemn me, without hearing my story.

BEAST. Why, steal, rose?

JEAN LOUIS. I didn't know . . . I thought . . . I couldn't . . . I looked . . I . . .

BEAST *growls.*

BEAST'S MAN. Master, doesn't under, under, understand a word.

JEAN LOUIS. I'm not, a thief, Beast. I took the rose, as a, gift, for Beauty.

BEAST. Beauty?

BEAST *growls softly.*

JEAN LOUIS. My youngest daughter.

BEAST *growls.*

BEAST. You. Steal. Must. Punish.

JEAN LOUIS. How, will you, punish me?

BEAST. Will . . . eat you!

JEAN LOUIS. My, God! Eat . . . me!?

BEAST'S MAN. Al, al, al, alive!

BEAST. Or, you, bring Beauty, here, be, Beast bride.

JEAN LOUIS. But my daughter, could never marry, a man of your status, Beast.

She must marry the son of a peasant. I'm poor. I can't even give my girls a decent dowry!

BEAST. I, seek no profit, merchant! She, is, herself a dowry.

JEAN LOUIS. But it's not . . .

BEAST. Eaten be, or daughter, give. Decide!

JEAN LOUIS (*aside*). To be eaten alive, or to give him my daughter! What kind of choice is that! I took you for a gentleman, Beast. A man of honour and reason. Surely, you will not behave like a tyrant.

How would it profit you, to eat me? How?

BEAST *roars.*

Let me plead my case! You are master of this, radiant place, where the carpets change colour with your thoughts, where tapestries teem with life and yet you would eat me, a guest, for plucking a rose?

BEAST *roars.*

Why, do you eat people, Beast? And why are you trying to steal my daughter?

BEAST. Because, Beast. Because, must.

JEAN LOUIS. Who could compel you to do anything? How many fathers have been eaten?

BEAST *roars.*

How many daughters, disappeared?

BEAST *roars.*

Why do you steal them, Beast? I demand, an answer?

BEAST. To be . . . to be . . .

JEAN LOUIS. Yes?

BEAST. Eaten be, or daughter give, decide!!! You have one month.

JEAN LOUIS. What?

BEAST. Go home, decide, come back.

JEAN LOUIS. I see.

BEAST. One. Month.

JEAN LOUIS. Why, thank you, Beast.

BEAST. Give, sacred, word.

JEAN LOUIS (*shows crossed fingers*). I'll return, in one month. Promise!

BEAST *turns away convinced.*

BEAST'S MAN. Don't c . . . c . . . cross . . . f . . . f . . . fingers, behind b . . . b . . . back.

BEAST *back, grabs* JEAN LOUIS.

BEAST. If you run, I, run faster. If you hide, I, will, find.

JEAN LOUIS. I give you my sacred word of honour, Beast, I will return in one month, to be eaten alive, or to give you my daughter.

BEAST. Tonight, guest. In morning, travel home, comfort, safety.

JEAN LOUIS *bows.* BEAST *kisses* JEAN LOUIS, *both cheeks.*

Show, room. Sleep well, merchant.

BEAST *offers rose to* JEAN LOUIS.

For Beauty.

BEAST *and* CHORUS *exit.*

BEAST'S MAN. Excellent! Follow me!

BEAST'S MAN *takes* JEAN LOUIS *to his room.*

BEAST'S MAN. Your roo . . . roo . . . room.

JEAN LOUIS. Very nice.

BEAST'S MAN. Food?

JEAN LOUIS. I'm not hungry.

BEAST'S MAN. In morning. Travel home.

JEAN LOUIS. Yes.

BEAST'S MAN. Bell, will ring.

JEAN LOUIS. An alarm call as it were.

BEAST'S MAN. Bell, will ring.

JEAN LOUIS. Right. Well. Thanks. (JEAN LOUIS *give* BEAST'S MAN *small polite bow.*)

BEAST'S MAN. Thank. You. (BEAST'S MAN *bows back deeply and starts to leave.*)

JEAN LOUIS. Can I ask you a question?

BEAST'S MAN. Any. Any. Anything!

JEAN LOUIS. What's your name?

BEAST'S MAN. B.B.B.B Beast's Man.

JEAN LOUIS. And. What, are you?

BEAST'S MAN. Mash . . . mash . . . mash . . . machine. Master, made, me, serve guests.

JEAN LOUIS. Oh. D'you have many guests?

BEAST'S MAN. Not, many.

JEAN LOUIS. No. I thought not.

BEAST'S MAN. Sleep. Well.

JEAN LOUIS. Um. I doubt it.

BEAST'S MAN. Sleep. Well.

JEAN LOUIS. Yes of course. Thank you. (JEAN LOUIS *bows.*)

BEAST'S MAN. Th . . . th . . . thank. You. (BEAST'S MAN *bows.*)

JEAN LOUIS. No. Thank you. (JEAN LOUIS *bows.*)

BEAST'S MAN. Thank you. (BEAST'S MAN *bows.*) Thank you. (BEAST'S MAN *bows.*) Thank you. (BEAST'S MAN *bows.*)

JEAN LOUIS. You seem to be stuck . . .

BEAST'S MAN. Mal . . . mal . . . mal. Thank (BEAST'S MAN *bows.*) Malfunction.

JEAN LOUIS. Can I help?

BEAST'S MAN. Hit me. Thank. (BEAST'S MAN *bows.*) Hit. Hit. Me. Hard!!

JEAN LOUIS. Right. (JEAN LOUIS *taps* BEAST'S MAN *gently and gingerly on the back, stands back.*)

BEAST'S MAN. Much. Th . . . th . . . thank. Much. HARDER.

JEAN LOUIS *hits* BEAST'S MAN *very hard. Big number from* BEAST'S MAN, *physical and verbal.*

Shhhhh . . . gggrrrr . . . ugu ugu . . . Plu, plu, plu . . . BBllll. Shtong!

Pause.

JEAN LOUIS. Is that better?

BEAST'S MAN. Thank you. (BEAST'S MAN *bows.*)

JEAN LOUIS. Oh, no! Still stuck?

BEAST'S MAN. Repair, suck, suck, suck . . . suck . . . suck . . . Successful!!!

JEAN LOUIS. Oh, right!!! Excellent!!!

BEAST'S MAN. Night. Merchant.

JEAN LOUIS. Good night! Beast's Man.

BEAST'S MAN *becomes clock,* JEAN LOUIS *gives big yawn.*

Will I be eaten alive? (*Yawns and big stretch.*)

Or will I lose my daughter? (*Yawns.*) Can't think. (*Yawns.*). Too tired. Too hard. (JEAN LOUIS *yawns and falls asleep.)*

Bell rings.

BEAST'S MAN. Morning!

JEAN LOUIS. Good morning.

BEAST'S MAN. Sleep, well?

JEAN LOUIS. No, no not a wink, you daft robot.

BEAST'S MAN. Sleep well?

BEAST'S MAN. Yes! Yes, surprisingly well, thank you.

BEAST'S MAN. Breakfast?

JEAN LOUIS. You know, I wouldn't mind a bite. A little nibble that is.

BEAST'S MAN *pulls cup from jacket, biscuits in saucer.*

JEAN LOUIS. Chocolate! Biscuits!

Enter WITCH.

And who are you?

WITCH. I am a witch.

JEAN LOUIS. Oh, hello, witch.

WITCH. I bring a present from the Master!!

Enter BEAST'S HORSE. *She stamps.*

This is Beast's horse!

BEAST'S HORSE *stamps feet in salute.*

BEAST'S MAN. She fly faster, than, the win . . . win . . . win . . . win

JEAN LOUIS *whacks* BEAST'S MAN *hard.*

Cheers. She flies, faster than, the, wind.

WITCH. If you bring Beauty, she must come in full knowledge of what awaits her here, nothing must be hidden.

JEAN LOUIS. Right.

WITCH. You may not force her. She must come of her own free will.

JEAN LOUIS. Right.

WITCH. It's time.

JEAN LOUIS. I can't ride that creature.

WITCH. You must. Just say. 'Take me to where I must go'.

BEAST'S HORSE *stamps, she's ready to go.* JEAN LOUIS *mounts her. He can't speak.*

JEAN LOUIS. 'Take me, to where, I must go.'

Music. Dance. JEAN LOUIS*'s journey home. Terrifying and exhilarating. Fast and furious as they cut through the clouds, abruptly pace changes and they float, gliding on currents of air.* BEAST'S HORSE *explodes.*

Scene Four: Beauty to the Palace

JEAN LOUIS *thrown into action and* HELENE, *narrating.* CHORUS *as country.*

JEAN LOUIS. What use is a month?

HELENE. The merchant was troubled!

JEAN LOUIS. I should have forced that monster to eat me on the spot, then there'd have been a speedy end to this hideous mess!

HELENE. But he couldn't help thinking . . .

JEAN LOUIS. What would Beauty say if she knew the full story?

HELENE. You see, he couldn't help feeling . . .

JEAN LOUIS. Getting married is not quite the same as being eaten alive!

HELENE. So he couldn't help wondering . . .

JEAN LOUIS. Would Beauty marry Beast . . . to save her father's life?

HELENE. What father wouldn't wonder thus?

JEAN LOUIS. No! I can't ask her that! I'll enjoy this month with my children. I'll embrace them, give them my blessing and prepare them for my departure. And when the month is up I'll return to the Palace and give myself to the Beast! There we are! A decent solution! I am resolved!

HELENE *hooks up the house.*

HELENE. And then, he saw . . . his home . . .

Music. House emerges. JEAN LOUIS, *overwhelmed. Enter* KIDS *from fields.*

ANDRE. Papa!?

PHILLIPE. You came back . . .

ANDRE. Alive . . .

EMILE. Papa?

MARIE CLARE. Where's my present?

VERONIQUE. Exactly!

JEAN LOUIS *finally turns and sees his children.*

JEAN LOUIS. Children. How you've grown . . .

VERONIQUE. What did you expect us to do, shrink!

MARIE CLARE. You've been away fourteen months! (MARIE CLARE *is about to cry.*)

VERONIQUE (*with a little note book, she's been counting off the minutes*).Twenty eight minutes, three hours and two days . . .

JEAN LOUIS. Oh, my little ones.

Music. Big reunion. BEAUTY *stands away.*

BEAUTY. Father!?

JEAN LOUIS. Beauty? (*Pause.*) You asked for a rose!? (*Pause.*) Take it.

JEAN LOUIS *holds out the rose to* BEAUTY, *who doesn't move.*

BEAUTY. What's happened?

JEAN LOUIS. It will cost your father dear.

BEAUTY. I don't understand. (*Pause.*)

MARIE CLARE. Is she the only one whose gonna get a present!?

Pause, KIDS *look at* JEAN LOUIS. *He is staring at* BEAUTY *but says nothing.*

VERONIQUE. Exactly. Well, that just about takes the cake . . .

MARIE CLARE. And puts the cherry on the biscuit tin!

ANDRE. Not now girls.

VERONIQUE. Where's my hand cream?!

MARIE CLARE. And my new dress.

PHILLIPE. Shut it!! (PHILLIPE *about to snap. Everyone is very upset.*)

VERONIQUE. My lacy gloves?!

MARIE CLARE. My lipstick!

EMILE. Witches!

ANDRE *restrains* EMILE *from attacking* SISTERS.

ANDRE. Let's all calm down now shall . . .

VERONIQUE *and* MARIE CLARE. What about, me, me, me . . .

ANDRE. We're all a bit churned up because papa's just . . .

VERONIQUE *and* MARIE CLARE. What about, ME!!!!!!!!!

Silence. KIDS *spent.* JEAN LOUIS *and* BEAUTY *still staring.*

BEAUTY. Father! What happened!!?

JEAN LOUIS *and* KIDS *into position to listen.*

HELENE. And the merchant told them his whole story . . .

EMILE. You found your ship?!!

JEAN LOUIS. All my dreams came true!!

HELENE. Told them their fortune was lost.

GIRLS. My dowry!!!

JEAN LOUIS. I won the case!

HELENE. Told of his cold night in the forest.

PHILLIPE. You slept in a tree!

JEAN LOUIS. My life was spared.

HELENE. Told of his first glimpse of the palace.

ANDRE. Completely, translucent . . .

JEAN LOUIS. Invisible and visible all at once.

HELENE. And the pathway of pearls . . .

EMILE. Orange blossom and fruit!?

JEAN LOUIS. It doesn't make sense?!

HELENE. And the golden stairs . . .

PHILLIPE. You were above the clouds?

JEAN LOUIS. Right next to the sun . . .

HELENE. And the magical rooms.

MARIE CLARE. Tapestries with animals?

JEAN LOUIS. Flapping in fabric.

HELENE. And the carpet of dreams . . .

VERONIQUE. Carpets can't dream!!

JEAN LOUIS. It turned pink with my thoughts!!

HELENE. He told them of his, ecstatic liberation . . .

BEAUTY. You were dancing with butterflies!!?

JEAN LOUIS. I was alive! I was happy! I was free!

HELENE. Then he told them about the Rose.

ALL. Huh!!

MARIE CLARE *snatches the rose greedily from* JEAN LOUIS. VERONIQUE *sniffs it.*

HELENE. And the witch!!

ALL. OOH!

HELENE. And the Beast!

ALL. No!

Rose is passed fast along the line to BEAUTY *at the end.*

HELENE. Then he told them of his promise to return in one month to be eaten alive!!?!

KIDS. No, papa.!!!

All at once, in a babble of rage and fear.

PHILLIPE. We won't let you go!

VERONIQUE. She's so horribly selfish!

EMILE. My sword is sharp, papa!

ANDRE. We will defend you!

MARIE CLARE. Papa, you can't leave me!

JEAN LOUIS. Mes enfants!!

Silence.

VERONIQUE. It's all her fault

HELENE. He told them of his promise to return, or to give Beauty to the Beast, to be his bride.

BOYS. No!!! (*All speak at once, overlapping.*)

EMILE. I'll go in her place!

MARIE CLARE. He won't marry a boy!

PHILLIPE. Don't even think about it Beauty!

VERONIQUE. She's killing our papa!

ANDRE. Beast is a tyrant!

JEAN LOUIS. Ça suffit!

Silence.

MARIE CLARE. Why didn't she ask for a normal kind of present!

BEAUTY. I asked for the rose. I'll go to the palace.

JEAN LOUIS. I won't let you, Beauty. What father would!

BEAUTY. To save your life! What daughter wouldn't!

JEAN LOUIS. You can't sacrifice yourself for me . . .

BEAUTY. If I marry Beast I'll be the wife of a rich and powerful man, the mistress of a magical palace!

JEAN LOUIS. Beauty?!!

BEAUTY. It's my duty!

BOYS. No!

BEAUTY. My destiny!

BOYS. No!

BEAUTY. My fate!

VERONIQUE. Well, that seems like a reasonable solution!

MARIE CLARE. Absolutely!!

VERONIQUE. And think about this Beast Girl, when the glamorous wedding is over and the guests have all gone home, this cannibal is sure to eat you up and when you're chewed and cracked and squirted out the other end . . .

VERONIQUE *and* MARIE CLARE. Err!

VERONIQUE. We'll have papa, all to ourselves!

BOTH. Hah!! Hah!! Hah!!

PHILLIPE *and* EMILE. Now!

VERONIQUE. Ah!!

PHILLIPE *and* EMILE *force* VERONIQUE *to the ground tie her and gag her.*

ANDRE. Brothers. Is brutality the only response you can summon up to resolve this conflict!?

MARIE CLARE. Papa!! Look what they're doing to Veronique . . .

PHILLIPE *and* EMILE. Now!

MARIE CLARE. Ah!

PHILLIPE *and* EMILE *grab* MARIE CLARE, *begin to tie her up, stop as* ANDRE *talks.*

ANDRE. Is oppression going to solve this problem in the long run?!

MARIE CLARE. Exactly, no brain bully boys, untie me or I'll cut you up!

ANDRE. Right. Let me give you a hand with that! (*He ties* MARIE CLARE*'s wrists.*)

JEAN LOUIS. Beauty, we'll spend this month together and then I'll go to the palace and give myself to the Beast!

BOYS. No!!

JEAN LOUIS. I'm going!!

BOYS. No!!

BEAUTY. I'm going!

BOYS. No!!

Music. JEAN LOUIS *and* BOYS *sleep.* BEAUTY *contemplates rose. Dance.*

HELENE. The month passed slowly and painfully. Every day the merchant tried to change his daughter's mind. Everyday she was resolute.

JEAN LOUIS *putting on his boots. On the morning when somebody had to leave for the palace . . .*

JEAN LOUIS. It's time . . .

HELENE. Beauty, said nothing.

JEAN LOUIS. I'm going, Beauty!

HELENE. Beauty, said nothing.

JEAN LOUIS. I've lived my life, yours has only just begun. (*Pause.*)

ANDRE. Beauty! Say something! (*Pause.*)

PHILLIPE. I know a cave in the mountains, behind a waterfall, it's huge! We'll run away together, all of us, and live in there.

BEAUTY. If you run, he will run faster!! If you hide, he will find.

ANDRE. He smells of the blood and rotting flesh of his victims.

BEAUTY. Why would he kill me if he wants me for his Bride!

EMILE. If you go, he'll eat you alive!!!

BEAUTY. It will be a speedy death!

JEAN LOUIS. He can barely utter a sentence . . .

BEAUTY. Yet he kissed you on both checks.

PHILLIPE. He grunts like an animal in a field . . .

BEAUTY. You said that he was a magician who ruled a magical palace . . .

JEAN LOUIS. He's a cannibal who will devour you . . .

BEAUTY. A place that softened your heart and freed your soul.

JEAN LOUIS. Beauty. I am your father. I love you. I must, nurture you, in all things, defend you from all harm. These are the sacred duties of a father. I have no choice. You live in my heart!

BEAUTY. You have protected me. Nurtured me. Loved me. And I will always feel blessed to have been your daughter. Now I must be free. Time to give the final gift, papa. Give me up. Let me go.

Enter BEAST'S HORSE, *stamping, terrifying. The* FAMILY, *except for* BEAUTY *and* JEAN LOUIS, *cower.*

ANDRE. What's this?

JEAN LOUIS. Beast's Horse! Come to collect me!

VERONIQUE *has wriggled gag off.*

VERONIQUE (*whispers*). Help me get these ropes off sis!

MARIE CLARE (*whispers*). Sure!

BEAST'S HORSE *stamps her feet, she's demanding action.*

JEAN LOUIS. Farewell. (*He can't move.*)

BEAUTY. I'm going. (*She can't move*). Goodbye.

BEAUTY *goes.* BROTHERS *stop her.*

BOYS. We won't let you go!

JEAN LOUIS. That's it. Hold her fast.

JEAN LOUIS *goes.* PHILLIPE *and* EMILE *stop him.*

BOYS. We won't let you go!

JEAN LOUIS. Unhand me.

BEAUTY (*fighting* ANDRE). Let me go.

PHILLIPE *and* EMILE. Hold her tight!!!

JEAN LOUIS. I've given my word.

JEAN LOUIS *is fighting* PHILLIPE *and* EMILE.

PHILLIPE *and* EMILE. Won't let you go!!

JEAN LOUIS. My sacred word!!

BEAUTY. Arrh! (BEAUTY *slips away from* ANDRE.)

ANDRE. Beauty, come back!

VERONIQUE. Now, we help her get on the horse!

PHILLIPE *and* EMILE. Andre!

ANDRE *collapses.* EMILE *and* PHILLIPE *let go of* JEAN LOUIS. BEAUTY *jumps on horse.*

BEAUTY. Take me to . . .

PHILLIPE *leaps up and stops* BEAUTY*'s mouth.*

PHILLIPE. Stop!!

BEAUTY *and* PHILLIPE *struggle on floor.* BEAUTY *slips out of* PHILLIPE*'s grasp. Faces* EMILE.

EMILE. You won't get past me, sister!

VERONIQUE. Let's knock 'em down, sister.

MARIE CLARE *and* VERONIQUE *tackle* EMILE, BEAUTY *gets to* BEAST'S HORSE.

BEAUTY. Take me to . . .

JEAN LOUIS *leaps up and grabs* BEAUTY. BOYS *stand between* BEAUTY *and* BEAST'S HORSE.

JEAN LOUIS. Stop.

BEAUTY *and* JEAN LOUIS *tumble.* BEAUTY *springs up.* BOYS *stand in her way.*

BOYS. You won't get past us, Beauty!

VERONIQUE. Prepare to die!

MARIE CLARE *and* VERONIQUE *tackle* BOYS, *gag them,* BEAUTY *gets to* BEAST'S HORSE.

VERONIQUE. Just say the words, blob!

VERONIQUE *and* MARIE CLARE. And never, never, come back!!

BEAUTY. Take me to where I must go.

Music. BEAST'S HORSE *takes off.*

The Journey to the Palace. The dance builds to a mighty climax. BEAUTY *runs downstage centre, holding rose in her fist.*

BEAUTY. I'm not afraid, to live my life, whatever that may bring!

BEAUTY *runs into Palace. Artillery, bagpipes. A big roar from* BEAST.

Blackout.

End of Act One.

ACT TWO

Scene One: Beauty's First Day

Music. Drumming. Curtain up. BEAUTY *kneeling with rose. Beast watches.* WITCH *and* CHORUS *sing, harmonising with* BEAUTY*'s lament.*

WITCH. Beauty didn't sleep a wink on her first night in the Palace of the Beast.

BEAUTY.

Song Of Lament

O maman, ma chère maman,
Tu m'as quitté, tu es partie,
Tu ne viens pas quand je pleurs,
Je cherche en vain mon âme soeur.
O maman ma chère maman,
Il n'y a personne pour me recomforter.

Music. Enter MAID *(played by* HELENE).

BEAUTY. Who are you!?

MAID. I am, your maid!

BEAUTY. Have you come to take me to the Beast?

MAID. I am, your maid!

Music. Enter FURNITURE.

BEAUTY. What are these things?

MAID. Furniture!?

FURNITURE. Welcome! Beauty!

BEAUTY. Welcome!? Furniture?!

MAID. Shall I, comb your hair?

BEAUTY. I don't think . . .

MAID. Could do with it!

Music. MAID *points.* BEAUTY *goes to* VANITY TABLE.

VANITY TABLE: Welcome! Beauty! (VANITY TABLE *passes brush to* BEAUTY.)

BEAUTY. Welcome?! Table?!

MAID *brushes hair firmly.*

Not so hard, please!

MAID. I am your, maid!

BEAUTY. Ow!!

Maid hits a knot. BEAUTY *jumps up.*

Be careful.

MAID. Sorry! My, first day.

BEAUTY. Me too.

BEAUTY *sits, slowly.* MAID *brushes less vigorously.*

MAID. What, lovely, hair, you have.

BEAUTY. Thank you. Ow! (*Another painful tangle.* BEAUTY *up very fast.*)

MAID. You should brush it, more often.

Music, WARDROBE *forward.*

WARDROBE. Welcome! Beauty!

BEAUTY. Welcome?! Wardrobe?!

MAID. Open!

Music. WARDROBE *opens, hands* BEAUTY *clothes and shoes.*

BEAUTY. A dress and a pair of shoes!?

MAID. What you expect, it's a wardrobe?

BEAUTY. But are these for me, maid!?

FURNITURE. Of course!

MAID. Beast made, dress for you, made me, for you.

FURNITURE. Beast!

Music. WARDROBE *retreats.* SCREEN *advances, closed position.*

SCREEN. Welcome! Beauty!

BEAUTY. Welcome! Screen!

MAID. Open!

Music. SCREEN *opens.* MAID *tries to grab* BEAUTY*'s dress.*

BEAUTY. I can manage, thank you . . .

MAID. I am, your maid!

BEAUTY. Okay.

Music. BEAUTY *and* MAID *go behind* SCREEN. WITCH *comes forward.*

BEAUTY. Could you do the buttons, please?

MAID. I am, your maid!

BEAUTY. Ow!! Be careful.

MAID. Stay, still.

WITCH. Welcome! Beauty!

BEAUTY *pops head over screen.*

BEAUTY. Who are you?!

WITCH. I am the witch.

BEAUTY. Have you come to take me to the Beast?

WITCH. I will be your guide and tutor in the palace. Here you will live a life of work and order. You will rise each morning at six, I will visit you for meditation and blessing, the rest of your day will be divided equally between study and palace exploration.

BEAUTY. What's meditation?

WITCH. Listening to the words that grow out of silence.

WITCH *points,* BEAUTY *sits.*

I will bring down the light.

Blessing dance.

BEAUTY. I feel . . . full of light.

WITCH. All beings contain the light. It is hidden. Inside. It must be revealed. This is my work.

Music. Enter BEAST'S MAN.

BEAUTY. B . . . B . . . B . . . Beast's Man! My father met you! Mal, mal, malfunction.

FURNITURE. Uhrr! (FURNITURE *smiles, sneeringly.*)

BEAST'S MAN. Speaking, function, fixed thanks! Uhrr! (BEAST'S MAN *glares at* FURNITURE.)

Music. BEAST'S MAN *opens a slot in his chest. Takes out an invite.*

From the master!

BEAUTY. Thank you! Excuse me. (BEAUTY *goes upstage to open and read.*)

BEAST'S MAN. Who are, you?

MAID. Beauty's Maid. Beast, made me.

BEAST'S MAN. Made us all, buttercup. Question is, are you, maid, for me?

MAID. Cheeky, monkey.

BEAST'S MAN. Let's, meet, later. Just the two.

MAID. No, chance!

FURNITURE. Uhrr. (BEAST'S MAN *gestures at* FURNITURE.)

BEAUTY. Beast wants me to join him for supper, at eight o'clock.

BEAST'S MAN. Answer?

BEAUTY. Tell him . . . Tell him, I accept. (BEAUTY *hands invite back to* BEAST'S MAN.)

BEAST'S MAN. To. The. Master!

Music. BEAST'S MAN *hurls invite, it flies out of room.*

WITCH. Until then Beauty you are free to explore the palace.

BEAST'S MAN. Recommend Room, Of, Mirrors!!

BEAUTY. What's that?

MAID. Big room? Lots of mirrors?

BEAST'S MAN (*aside*). Clever clogs! (*Thumbs up from* MAID. *To* BEAUTY.) It's, really, really, good!

BEAUTY. How do we get there?

WITCH. Close your eyes.

Music. CHORUS *into position.* CHORUS *and* WITCH *sing.*

WITCH *and* CHORUS.
To the East of the sun to the West of the moon
Carry us to our chosen room.

A spinning, singing, round, as spell is wound.

ALL (*sing*).
East. West. Sun. Moon.
Carry Beauty. Chosen room!

Take off. Exit CHORUS *and* FURNITURE, *spinning, others big step forward.*

BEAST'S MAN. The Room of Mirrors!!!

BEAUTY. Wow!

The room is an ultra-violet fantasy.

MAID (*aside*). Smart move, metal man!

BEAST'S MAN (*aside*). Stick with me I'll show you a good time.

MAID (*aside*). Yeah, yeah, sure.

Music. Enter CHORUS *with mirror frames.*

SECTION ONE

Music. Slow and heavy. Four mirror frames (two metres wide and three high) shuffle on in symmetrical pattern, two upstage left and two right. When fully on stage big change of rhythm. Music fast, light. Mirrors run downstage centre and form a wall across the front of the stage. Music, melodic and playful with sudden stops. MAID *and* BEAST'S MAN *enjoy mirrors in a playful, comedic way. Tongue sticking out, face pulling. Heroic posing for* BEAST'S MAN. *Glamorous posing for* MAID. WITCH *and* BEAUTY *contemplative. They are seeing into themselves in mirror.*

SECTION TWO

Music changes. Insistent, urgent, fast. Mirrors rotate, then travel to create an up and down stage corridor. Other actors have travelled upstage centre as mirrors have moved. They run, through the mirrors. BEAUTY *and* WITCH *first.* BEAST'S MAN *and* MAID *following. They are jumping through each mirror, musical crash at each penetration. They travel downstage centre. Mirrors have created new shape. A line across centre stage. Characters weave through mirrors jumping and smashing as they go. At upstage centre rose door opens. Mirrors into position around upstage centre door. Door reveals a mysterious stranger, dressed in mirror:* KING OF MIRRORS. *The four characters dance an elegant quadrille, with the four large mirrors.*

SECTION THREE

Big change. Travelling music. Mirrors line up two each side of stage, creating archways off into wings. The KING OF MIRRORS *leads* BEAUTY *off upstage right.* BEAST'S MAN *leads* MAID *off downstage left.* KING OF MIRRORS *and* BEAUTY *enter downstage right, cross, spin and lift mid stage centre, exit upstage left.* MAID *and* BEAST'S MAN *enter downstage left. As he tries to kiss her, she whacks him, they exit upstage right. Enter* KING OF MIRRORS *and* BEAUTY. *Downstage left they dance, and exit upstage right. Downstage right* BEAST'S MAN *and* MAID *try to dance romantically, toes get trodden on, trips, pratfalls. Rose door opens. Enter* KING OF MIRRORS, *who disappears out of door. All wave goodbye.* BEAUTY *rushes to the rose door as it closes.* BEAST'S MAN *leads* MAID *away as* BEAUTY*'s back is turned.*

SECTION FOUR

CHORUS *enter with smaller single mirrors. They dance around her. She looks into the mirrors they look into her. A number of shapes are danced into. Waves of mirror. Cascades of mirror.* BEAUTY *and room are released and really enjoying dancing together. This section climaxes with the mirrors all being placed over* BEAUTY*'s head. The mirrors form a geometric pattern on the floor.* BEAUTY *discovers a locket, at her feet. She ponders it. Re-enter* BEAST'S MAN *and* MAID, *she looking shy, he very cocky.*

BEAUTY. Where have you two been?

BEAST'S MAN. Exploring!

BEAUTY. Look at this.

MAID. Lovely, locket. What's, inside.

BEAUTY *tentatively opens locket.*

BEAUTY. An inscription . . .

BEAST'S MAN. Breathe on it and rub.

She does.

(*Aside.*) Happy, honeysuckle?

MAID (*aside*). Quite, happy.

The locket sings and glows. All gather around BEAUTY *and locket.*

LOCKET. Beauty. Beauty. Beauty. See with more than your eyes. See with more than your eyes. See with more than your eyes.

BEAUTY (*to* WITCH). What does it mean?

The clock chimes eight.

WITCH. It's eight o'clock.

BEAST (*off*). Beauty!

Set change to dining room. BEAST'S MAN *propels* BEAUTY. *Enter dining table, laden with food, wine, etc. Enter* BEAST. BEAUTY *terrified.*

BEAST. Beau . . . ty!

BEAUTY. Good. Evening!

BEAST *goes to* BEAUTY. *Sniffs at her for long time, like an animal.*

BEAUTY. I don't like this, Beast. It's rude and I'd like you to stop. Please. Go back to your place.

BEAST *looks her in the face. Sniffs, goes.*

BEAST. Beau . . . ti . . . ful.

BEAUTY. Thank you.

BEAST *sits down. Soup tureen floats over to him.*

BEAUTY. How did that happen?

BEAST. Magic. Table. (BEAST *eating, bestially, noisily, passionately.*)

BEAUTY. Oh, dear.

BEAST *hears this, looks up confused.*

BEAST. What?

BEAUTY. Nothing. Enjoy . . . your soup.

BEAST *eats again, stops.*

BEAST. Sit. Eat.

BEAUTY. I'm not, hungry. (*Picks up bowl drinks more soup, stops.*)

BEAST. Why?

BEAUTY. My mouth is dry. My hands are shaking. I feel sick in the stomach. I don't think I could manage a mouthful.

BEAST *wipes hands clean on cloth, picks at his huge nails.*

BEAST. Frightened?

BEAUTY. I think it would be fair to say that I'm absolutely terrified.

BEAST. Why?

BEAUTY. I'm having dinner with . . . a creature, who threatened to eat my father and may at any moment choose to eat me.

BEAST. No, eat. (BEAST *is hurt at the implication.*)

BEAUTY. You're not going to eat me?

BEAST. Never. Not, eat, people.

BEAUTY. Why did you threaten to eat my father?

BEAST *growls, pause.*

It's a simple question. (*Pause.*) Answer me.

BEAST *roars.*

Why did you threaten to eat my father?

BEAST. Because Beast! Because must!

BEAUTY. That doesn't get us very far does it? You know I've had enough of this, Beast.

BEAST *roars.*

You may roar as much as you like, when I've finished speaking, until then I trust that you will do me the courtesy of listening. You have terrorised my family, Beast, made all our lives a misery. You threaten to kill my father, for the minor offence of stealing a rose . . .

BEAST *roars.*

And then you leave me little choice but to come here and live as a prisoner in your palace.

BEAST *roars.*

And you invite me to supper! As if I had any choice, Beast! What would have happened if I'd refused? Would witch have cast a spell on me or perhaps your man would have tied me up and dragged me here.

BEAST *roars.*

You are a tyrant, Beast! Nothing better than a playground bully.

BEAST *roars.*

Speak, words.

BEAST. Not want, hurt. (*Pause,*). Want, friend.

BEAUTY. Oh? Well, you have a strange way of making friends, I must say.

BEAST. I, am, a, fool!

BEAUTY. No. You are not a fool, Beast.

BEAST *growls.*

The world is full of men who claim to be wise but who act like fools!

BEAST *growls.*

If at times you behave in a foolish manner, then at least you have the good sense to recognise your folly.

BEAST *growls.*

You can't just resort to making these inarticulate noises. If you want to make friends, we must exchange words, this roaring, strikes me as plain bad manners and I wish you'd stop.

BEAST *roars. Anger and frustration have turned in, he's hunched up.*

I hope you're not succumbing to self-pity about . . . whatever it is, that's troubling you. Self-pity is most unattractive and most unproductive! (*Pause.*) Where is he, Beast? The kind and gentle man, who made me a beautiful dress, who fitted new shoes on my feet and left a rose on my pillow?

BEAST *growls.*

Answer, Beast, or I shall be forced to withdraw from this sumptuous feast and return to my room.

BEAST. No words. To speak . . . my . . . heart.

BEAUTY. Well, you may use a limited vocabulary Beast, but your thoughts, when you express them, emerge with clarity and power.

BEAST. Bumbling. Words!!!

BEAUTY. Granted, your conversational style is unconventional but it is honest. Many men employ clever words and elaborate sentences to cover up vile intentions. Your words, suggest an open, honest heart. Come and sit down and please don't upset yourself with the thought that I think less of you for the way you talk. Let's have no more roaring and growling and lying on the floor in the middle of supper!

BEAST *goes to* BEAUTY *and holds out a rose.*

BEAST. For, you.

BEAUTY. Your roses are so perfect.

BEAST. Rose. Garden. First thing, I make, here.

BEAUTY. I see.

BEAST (*holds out her chair*). Sit?

BEAUTY. Thank you.

BEAST. Eat?

BEAUTY. Yes, please, I'm starving. I think I'll have some soup.

Music. Soup tureen lifts and pours itself into BEAUTY*'s bowl, she sips, then gulps it down, greedily.*

BEAST. Good?

BEAUTY. It's too good to eat with a silly spoon. (*Throws spoon, drinks.*)

BEAST. Enjoy?

BEAUTY. The best!!

BEAST. More?

BEAUTY. No, I want some of that roast beef. (*Platter floats.*)

BEAST. Beef. (*Beef floats over to* BEAST.)

BEAUTY. Let's eat. (*Squelch into beef with fingers.*) Good?

BEAST. Yeah! Beef!

Both eat greedily with fingers.

BEAUTY. Did you prepare this meal Beast and make this table and the magical rooms and the mechanical servants?

BEAST. For you. (*A sauce boat floats up from the table.*) Sauce?

BEAUTY. Horseradish, yummy!!

They eat in happy silence.

BEAST. Happy. Now.

BEAUTY. You are a riddle Beast, like two things, in the same skin, a civilised gentleman and a primitive creature, the gentleman ashamed of the animal and the animal confused by the gent. Is it terribly confusing being you, Beast? Do you live in awful pain? I think you suffer deeply! Well. Let's have some dessert!

BEAST *points to fruit dish.*

In here?

BEAUTY *lifts lid, it's full of strawberries.*

Strawberries!

Closes, opens, now full of figs.

Figs!

BEAST *opens again. The food changes again.*

Pomegranates. A self-replenishing fruit dish. What a splendid idea. What would you prefer? Strawberries?

BEAST. With cream! (BEAST *digs hand in cream and dollops it on plate.*)

BEAUTY. Oh, my. I'll have the same as you. (BEAUTY *puts hands in cream.*)

BEAUTY. Why did you want me to come here, Beast?

BEAST. To be. To be, my, bride.

BEAUTY. Oh, yes. Right! Of course, I have known of your intentions towards me in this respect for some time Beast and I have considered your proposal deeply.

BEAST. And . . .

BEAUTY. I believe that any marriage bought about through force or fear could never be happy . . .

BEAST. And . . .

BEAUTY. I think that marriage should be entered into by two souls who share a deep respect, two souls who are blessed with a profound natural attraction one for the other . . .

BEAST. And . . .

BEAUTY. I will only marry you when I can put my hand on my heart and know that it is full of love and full of joy. If that day comes I will consent to be your wife . . . and if it never comes, then you may torture me in your darkest dungeon or threaten me with imminent death but I will never marry you.

Pause.

BEAST. No words, till, then.

BEAUTY. No words, till then. I need a glass of water . . .

A water jug floats to BEAUTY. *It pours her a long cold glass. She drinks it in one,* BEAST *watches transfixed.* BEAUTY *yawns.*

BEAUTY. I didn't sleep very well last night.

BEAST *waves, table exits. Offers* BEAUTY *hand, lifts her gently.*

Thank you.

BEAST. Tomorrow?

BEAUTY. Let's meet tomorrow! I have enjoyed our supper.

BEAST. You, beau . . . ti . . ful. (*Gives her the rose.*)

BEAUTY. Good night, Beast.

BEAST. Good night. Beauty.

Music. BEAST *summons* BEAST'S MAN*, he arrives.* BEAST *exit.* BEAST'S MAN *transports* BEAUTY *to her bedroom.* BED *and* FURNITURE *enter.*

BEAST'S MAN. Room.

BEAUTY. Thank you.

BEAST'S MAN. Night, mistress.

BEAUTY. Good night. (*Yawns.*)

BEAST'S MAN. Sleep. Well.

BEAUTY. I will.

BEAST'S MAN *bows, begins to exit but hides in wardrobe.*

WARDROBE. Oi!

BEAUTY. What was that?

MAID. Dress off. Nightie on.

BEAUTY. Right.

SCREEN. Evening! Mistress!

BEAUTY. Evening, screen.

MAID. Open!

Music. SCREEN *opens,* BEAUTY *gets changed,* MAID *to wardrobe, whispers.*

Open!

WARDROBE. Don't like this, at all.

MAID. Open, I'll get him, out.

WARDROBE. Good plan.

Music. WARDROBE *door opens,* BEAST'S MAN*'s head pops out.*

BEAST'S MAN. Hello, tiger lily.

MAID. Get out!

BEAST'S MAN. Kiss me, daffodil?

MAID. Out!

Maid pulls, BEAST'S MAN *slips her grip,* MAID *tumbles back, springs back up.*

We're over, metal man.

BEAST'S MAN. Only just, begun, bluebell.

MAID. Got to help, mistress.

BEAST'S MAN. If you leave, I'll, k . . . k . . . k . . . kill, myself.

VANITY TABLE. Don't fall for that.

MAID. Do you love me so much?

FURNITURE. Too late.

BEAST'S MAN. Love you, to bits apple blossom. Come in and cuddle!

WARDROBE. No way!

BEAST'S MAN. Shut it! Or I'll unscrew your panels.

BEAUTY. Maid?! (*Feeling top of* SCREEN.) Where's my night dress?

MAID. Coming, mistress. (MAID *moves to assist* BEAUTY.)

BEAST'S MAN. Don't go! (*Steps out of* WARDROBE *to recall* MAID.)

MAID. Nightie! Slippers! (*She hands* BEAUTY *her slippers.*)

FURNITURE. Witch!

FURNITURE *points.* BEAST'S MAN *tries to get back in* WARDROBE. WARDROBE *screams. Shuts doors.* BEAST'S MAN *runs, tries* VANITY TABLE, *screams. Hides behind* SCREEN.

MAID (*screams*). Not, behind there!!

Enter WITCH.

Good evening, witch.

WITCH. Good evening!

BEAUTY. Good evening, Witch!

WITCH. How was supper?

BEAUTY. The food was delicious.

WITCH. And the conversation?

BEAUTY. Improved dramatically, after a tricky start, I'd say.

BEAUTY *comes from behind the screen.*

He's such a fascinating creature. I've never met anyone remotely like him.

WITCH. He is unique.

BEAUTY. We are going to meet, tomorrow evening, for supper.

WITCH. I see. Now. Prayers, before bed.

BEAUTY *kneels to say her prayers.*

BEAUTY (*yawns*). I'm not sure I've much left to say.

WITCH. Be silent and sincere. The words will come.

BEAUTY. Why is silence so important to you, witch?

WITCH. Everything comes out of silence.

BEAUTY. How can I thank you for all that you are giving me?

WITCH. You are receiving. That is enough.

Music. BEAUTY *says her prayers.*

BEAUTY. Today I feel that I have– (*Yawns.*) – changed so much.

WITCH. You must prepare for great leaps and discoveries in the palace.

It's time for bed. You've had quite a day. Good night, Beauty.

BEAUTY. Good night. Witch.

Exit WITCH.

Night, Maid. (BEAUTY *yawns and gets into bed.*)

MAID. Night. Mistress.

BEAUTY. Night, wardrobe and (BEAUTY *yawns deeply.*) Why is screen still open?

SCREEN. Because. Beast's Man is . . . (*hiding behind me*).

MAID. Going to put oil, on screen's hinges, in the, morning.

SCREEN. But that's not . . . (*true at all, mistress*).

MAID. That's not, a problem.

SCREEN. But I didn't . . .

MAID. Screen's, a bit rusty, mistress.

BEAUTY (*yawns*). I'll see you all in the morning.

FURNITURE. Night, mistress.

BEAUTY *sleeps.* SCREEN *closes, revealing* BEAST'S MAN *crouching.*

BEAST'S MAN. That was close.

MAID. Made me lie to mistress!

BEAST'S MAN. Don't fret, bluebell.

FURNITURE. Made, maid, embarrass screen.

SCREEN *is crying.*

BEAST'S MAN. This will unscrew, anything!

BEAST'S MAN*'s screwdriver is out. All retreat.*

Turn round. Go to. Sleep.

FURNITURE. Careful, maid.

BEAST'S MAN. Errr.

BEAST'S MAN *chases* FURNITURE *upstage.*

Now we talk?

MAID. Not, now. Low on. Fuel.

BEAST'S MAN *offers* MAID *what looks like sweets.*

BEAST'S MAN. Fancy a boiled ball bearing, babe!?!

MAID. Umm!! (*She eats noisily, a very crunchy sound.*)

BEAST'S MAN. Drink!? (*He holds out a tube from his body.*)

MAID. Fill me up.

There is a working dial somewhere on her costume.

BEAST'S MAN. Petrol and paraffin, smoothie?

MAID. In here!

MAID *indicates head, he puts pipe in her headpiece.*

BEAST'S MAN. Better.

MAID. Much.

BEAST'S MAN. Flowers.

The magician's 'appearing bouquet' trick.

MAID (*smells flowers*). Thanks.

MAID *puts them in her headpiece.*

BEAST'S MAN. Nice. Now. Kiss?

MAID. What you take me for?

MAID *opens* BEAUTY*'s locket. It sings.*

LOCKET. Beauty.
Beauty.
Beauty.
See, with more than your eyes.
See, with more than your eyes.
See, with more than your eyes.

MAID. What's it, mean.

BEAST'S MAN. No idea. Want a present?

MAID. No.

BEAST'S MAN *pulls washer from inner workings.*

What's that?

BEAST'S MAN. Engagement ring!

MAID. It's washer from, your inner, drive shaft, propeller.

BEAST'S MAN. Will you marry me?

MAID. Okay!

BEAST'S MAN. Kiss, now?

MAID. Please!

They kiss several times.

BOTH. Uumm. Lovely.

MAID. Night. Night.

BEAST'S MAN. Night. Night.

Waving. MAID *sleeps. Music. Enter* WITCH. BEAUTY*'s bed rocks.* CHORUS *do passage of time dance, clock ticking out the years.*

WITCH. Every night for the next seven years at the same time and on the same spot, Beauty offered up her hopes and fears to the unknown. Every morning she practised her meditation and received her blessing and with each passing day she grew stronger and deeper and became more fully herself.

Music. Enter BEAUTY, *masked, dancing.*

Beauty soon overcame her fear of the Beast and in time she developed a deep affection for him, and he for her.

Enter BEAST, *dancing.*

They shared supper every evening without fail and they learned to listen to each other and to share in the way that only special friends can.

BEAUTY *and* BEAST *dance with* CHORUS *and furniture. The dance expresses the journey of their relationship from shyness and self consciousness, through conversation and getting to know each other, into confidence, relaxation and desire.* BEAST *learns from her grace and gentleness and* BEAUTY *acquires some of his passion and instinctual force. It is finally a full-blown romance. Dance ends, exit,* BEAUTY *and* BEAST.

You have seen Beauty's first day in the palace of the Beast, now we must show you the day that proved to be almost her last.

Exit WITCH.

Scene Two: The Penultimate Day

BEAUTY *in bed,* BEAST *watching.* CHORUS *create alarm clock.*

Clock Song.

Ma belle mignonne,
Ma belle mignonne.
Reveille-toi ma belle, open your eyes.
Ma belle mignonne, ma belle mignonne.
Wake up, wake up
Wake up, wake up.

Enter MAID, *carrying new dress,* FURNITURE *follows, re-covered in new fabric.*

MAID. Morning, mistress.

BEAUTY. Morning, maid.

Pause.

MAID. Must, begin . . .

BEAUTY. What?

MAID. The day . . .

BEAUTY. Of course.

Pause.

MAID. Mustn't, be late!

Pause.

Witch here, one minute! (*Consulting her nurse's watch.*)

BEAUTY. Sorry, maid!

Rose used as book mark. BEAUTY *descends ladder.*

BEAUTY. Open.

Music. BEAUTY *goes behind* SCREEN.

SCREEN. Morning, mistress.

BEAUTY. Morning screen. (*Taking nightie off.*) Did my books arrive?

MAID. Not, yet mistress!

BEAUTY *throws nightie over.*

Thanks. Beast sent, you, new dress! (MAID *puts dress on back of the screen.*)

BEAUTY. Thank you!

Music. Enter BEAST'S MAN *with a trolley full of books for* BEAUTY.

BEAST'S MAN. My, little watermelon!

MAID. Not, talking, to you!

BEAUTY. Is that my books?

BEAST'S MAN. Yes. Mistress.

BEAUTY. Put them on, table, please.

BEAST'S MAN *unloads.* MAID *checks books on* VANITY TABLE.

MAID. Alchemy! Algebra!

BEAST'S MAN. I don't, understand . . .

MAID. Apple bobbing!

BEAST'S MAN. What's going on . . .

MAID. Botany! Buddhism!

BEAST'S MAN. Tell me!

MAID. Bird Watching!

BEAST'S MAN. Pineapple . . . please . . .

MAID. Chemistry! Christianity!

BEAST'S MAN. It's not fair . . .

MAID. Cod Liver Oil Management!

BEAST'S MAN. What have I done?

BEAUTY *enters from behind* SCREEN.

BEAUTY. What do you think?

MAID. Really, really, lovely.

Enter WITCH, *prepares blessing.*

ALL. Morning, witch.

WITCH. Morning, everybody.

MAID. Demonology! Dermatology! Dog Biscuit Baking?

WITCH. What's happened, Beauty?

BEAUTY. Last night. I dreamt of my father. He was on his own, far out at sea, bobbing up and down in the waves and calling to me for help. I was somehow, floating, just above him as if I could fly, I stretched out my hand but I couldn't quite reach him and I watched as he slowly lost strength and began to swallow water, all the time I was stretching out, trying to reach him. Just as he was disappearing beneath the waves, I woke up.

WITCH. Dreams come and go, Beauty. Silence, is always present.

WITCH *and* CHORUS *poised to begin blessing and meditation.*

MAID. Egg Blowing! Egyptology! Euthanasia!

WITCH. Enough! I will bring down the light!

BEAUTY. I don't want to do any of this, witch! I want to go home and see my father!

WITCH. Only Beast can release you.

FURNITURE. Beast!

BEAUTY. Take me to him.

Pause.

Where is he?

WITCH. Making a new room for you.

BEAUTY. I want to see him, now.

WITCH. As you wish.

BEAUTY. There always seems to be another twist in the road.

WITCH. There is no end to the journey, Beauty. Follow me.

Music. BEAUTY, WITCH *and* CHORUS *exit in formation. Through rose door.*

FURNITURE. Oh, no

BEAST'S MAN. What's wrong?

FURNITURE. Beauty is leaving the palace.

BEAST'S MAN. Master, won't let her. What's wrong, with you, orange blossom?

MAID. Saw you. Flirting, in kitchen, with another, maid.

BEAST'S MAN. That er, that er, that er, mal, mal, mal function.

MAID *hits* BEAST'S MAN *very hard. He wobbles and vibrates again.*

Blu. Blu. Blu, Blu. Bloop. Cheers. That didn't mean a thing.

FURNITURE. Watch, him.

BEAST'S MAN. This is, between me and my, fiancée.

FURNITURE. Sorry.

FURNITURE *retreats upstage centre. Tries not to listen.*

BEAST'S MAN. She talks, to everyone, like that. Won't happen, again.

MAID. You're right. It won't.

BEAST'S MAN. Can you forgive, me?!

MAID. No.

BEAST'S MAN. Give me a chance. I'll do anything. Any, any, anything!

MAID. Presents are nice.

BEAST'S MAN. You want a present?

MAID. I was joking!

BEAST'S MAN. Name it.

MAID. Was, joking.

BEAST'S MAN. Really, really, love you!

MAID. I'd like, new dress! Been wearing this, thing, seven years. Beauty always gets new dress. And . . . And . . . And . . .

BEAST'S MAN. What?

MAID. Been wearing this washer seven years, as well. A very, very long engagement.

BEAST'S MAN. Come with me.

MAID. Where?

BEAST'S MAN. We'll get married in room of stories.

FURNITURE. Hurrah!

FURNITURE, BEAST'S MAN *and* MAID *exit as* WITCH *and* BEAUTY *and* CHORUS *enter. Empty room. Single industrial light. Trap opens downstage centre, intense light from inside, the inner workings of the palace. Hum of machines and technology.*

WITCH. Master! Master!

WITCH*'s voice echoes in the deep.*

BEAST'S MAN. Master, Beauty is with me.

BEAST'S *head in trap, wearing welding mask and holding a torch.*

BEAST. Here?

WITCH. This matter is urgent and unavoidable.

BEAST. Speak. Beauty.

BEAUTY. Beast. I want to go home!

BEAST. Home?

BEAUTY. I want to see my father. I miss him and I miss my family.

BEAST. Leave. Here?

BEAUTY. Only for a visit. In a month, I will return. To be with you.

BEAST. Will be, lonely, if you go.

BEAUTY. I must go.

BEAST. Not see you? Not hear you? How can I let you go. My, joy. My hope. My, happiness.

BEAUTY *runs into his embrace.*

WITCH. Patience. Beast.

BEAST. Beauty, mine. Not, go!

WITCH. Beauty is not yours.

BEAST *roars at* WITCH*, lashes out viciously at her.*

BEAST. Love. Her. Keep her.

WITCH. If you love her you will let her go!

Roars. Lashes out. Still clasping BEAUTY. BEAUTY *stands back from* BEAST*'s embrace, strokes him.*

BEAUTY. Here is my home. My hope. My happiness.

BEAUTY *stokes* BEAST*'s face.*

BEAST. Can, deny you, nothing.

BEAUTY. Thank you, Beast.

Music. BEAST *takes a ring from his finger.*

BEAST'S MAN. Take, this ring. When you travel, turn the stone, to face your palm, say: Over land, any land. Over sea, any sea. Take me, where my heart must be.

BEAUTY. I will return in one month.

BEAST. Farewell.

BEAUTY. Farewell.

A passionate embrace between BEAUTY *and* BEAST. WITCH *looks away.*

WITCH. You are free to go.

BEAUTY. Thank you witch. Goodbye.

WITCH. Goodbye, Beauty.

BEAUTY *stands, looks at ring, turns it round.*

BEAUTY. Over land, any land. Over sea, any sea. Take me to where my heart must be.

CHORUS, BEAUTY *and* WITCH (*singing*)
Over Land. Over Sea. Take me where. Heart must be.
Any land. Any sea. Must be where. Heart is free.
Must be where heart is free. Over land. Heart must be. Over sea.
Must be free. Must be free. Must be free. Must be free.
Heart must be. Heart must be. Heart must be. Free.

A wild storm breaks out and a whirlwind rages. BEAUTY, WITCH, CHORUS *all rotate. Tall house pops up to represent* BEAUTY*'s home.*

Scene Three: Home Again

Family farm, late September, warm evening, a pram. Enter JEAN LOUIS, *face covered in shaving suds.*

JEAN LOUIS. Are you a ghost come from the grave?

BEAUTY. I am your daughter.

JEAN LOUIS. My daughter died seven years ago . . .

BEAUTY. Helene, was my mother's name, she died when I was five years old and you Jean Louis are my father. (*Embrace. Bubbles.*)

JEAN LOUIS. Every morning, I prayed that Beast had spared your life and every night I feared that he had eaten you.

BEAUTY. Beast . . . is good . . . papa.

JEAN LOUIS. Let me wipe your face?

Enter PHILLIPE *and* ANDRE, *they see* BEAUTY.

PHILLIPE. Who's that with papa?

ANDRE. Beauty! (*He embraces* BEAUTY.) Beauty! Sister! My, sister!

BEAUTY. How's the universe, brother!

ANDRE. Oh, you know, continually expanding!

PHILLIPE. You can't keep her all to yourself. I want a go.

ANDRE, *hanky out.*

ANDRE. I'm really, really . . . (*Blows nose.*) Sorry. It's just . . . (*Blows.*) I'm so . . .

JEAN LOUIS. Now, then, Andre!

JEAN LOUIS *gives hanky, more blowing.*

BEAUTY. Andre, don't fall over . . .

ANDRE. Beauty! I don't do that anymore.

Baby crying. ANDRE *turns and falls.*

BEAUTY. Whose baby is that?

VERONIQUE (*off*). Shut that screaming brat up before I strangle it!

BEAUTY. Veronique?

Enter VERONIQUE *from house in a rage, plain and drab.*

VERONIQUE. Just, roll the pram into the river . . . Who's this?

BEAUTY. Your sister.

VERONIQUE. Thought you were dead!

BEAUTY. Apparently not.

VERONIQUE. I told you to never come back . . .

BEAUTY. And here I am . . .

Enter MARIE CLARE *with an overnight bag.*

MARIE CLARE. Hi, losers!

VERONIQUE. Sis! Blob's, back!

MARIE CLARE *sees* BEAUTY *for first time.*

MARIE CLARE. What d'you want?

BEAUTY. Nothing.

MARIE CLARE. The monster didn't eat you then?

BEAUTY. Sorry.

ANDRE. Marie Clare, please!

VERONIQUE. Leave her alone, farmer boy!

BEAUTY. Let's not argue!

Simultaneous, overlapping, arguments:

MARIE CLARE. Don't you start on me, bumpkin!

ANDRE. Well, what kind of welcome was that?

VERONIQUE. How dare she just, drop in on us like this.

JEAN LOUIS. She's your sister.

MARIE CLARE. Well, she's not welcome here.

PHILLIPE. More welcome than you.

BEAUTY. Family. Please!

They stop dead. Pause.

MARIE CLARE (*to* ANDRE). At least I can stand on my own two feet. (*Baby crying.*)

VERONIQUE. Tie a rock round it and throw it in the drink.

MARIE CLARE. Yeah right. I fancy a drink!

MARIE CLARE *and* VERONIQUE *exit.*

ANDRE (*rocking the pram*). Sh. Sh. It's alright, mummy's gone now.

BEAUTY. What's her name?

JEAN LOUIS. Madeleine.

BEAUTY. How old is she?

PHILLIPE. She'll be one, three weeks on Sunday.

BEAUTY. Who's the father?

PHILLIPE. The son of the mayor, in the village.

ANDRE. Veronique left him six weeks ago because he wouldn't buy her a new house. And the other monster . . .

JEAN LOUIS. Andre!

ANDRE. The other monster married a good-for-nothing soldier six years ago, three months after the wedding he went away to fight a war and hasn't been heard of since and who can blame him.

JEAN LOUIS. Andre, please!

ANDRE. Marie Clare claims she's still in love with him, she has a terrible reputation in the village.

JEAN LOUIS. She's unhappy, Andre.

ANDRE. She's a drunk, papa. Ssh now. Ssh.

BEAUTY. And what of you brothers? What's your story?

PHILLIPE. The farm stretches right down to the river.

All look out.

We make wine now.

JEAN LOUIS. The biggest wine growers in the region. Your brothers have worked hard.

ANDRE. Phillipe's been working hard, papa!

PHILLIPE. We did it together, Andre! He invented a bottling process that halved our costs and changed everything.

ANDRE. Yeah, but, y'know, it's not really what I want to be doing.

PHILLIPE. Andre should go to Paris and study astronomy.

ANDRE. Yes, well, Phillipe is working so hard that he's driven all the joy out of his life. He needs to take time off and start playing sport again.

JEAN LOUIS. Boys!

ANDRE. Phillipe hasn't yet managed to get married despite having been engaged for five years.

PHILLIPE. I'm desperate to get married, Andre!

ANDRE. So, what's holding you up.

Pause.

JEAN LOUIS. I'm happy tending the garden and pruning the roses.

BEAUTY. Where is Emile?

ANDRE. He locks himself away in his bunker night and day and thinks of nothing but inventing new kinds of exotic ice cream flavours.

PHILLIPE. He stopped washing two years ago.

ANDRE. We should seal up his silly bunker and force him to work in the vineyard. At least that way he'd get some fresh air and see the light of day.

Enter EMILE *from trap, in his apron.*

EMILE. Beauty!

BEAUTY. Emile!

EMILE. I got a machine for making ice cream!!!

PHILLIPE. Let's go inside!

EMILE. Tonight, it's ice cream on a stick!

JEAN LOUIS. Supper's ready!

EMILE. I've created a spring onion and icing sugar surprise! A lamb chop and lemon curd sorbet!

ANDRE. Emile!

EMILE. And my special for tonight is baked tadpole and smoked haddock, with boiled blackbird jelly and pigeon liver sauce! I don't think you will have tasted anything quite like it.

BEAUTY. Emile, that all sounds absolutely disgusting!

Music. All into house. VERONIQUE *enters, bottle of wine and two glasses.*

VERONIQUE. Sis, sis!

MARIE CLARE *enters, drunk and smoking a cigar.*

No one must hear what I've got to say to you! 'Cept you, of course. (*Pours.*) We've always hated blob, right from the very beginning. Always playing with the boys and trying to steal papa from us.

MARIE CLARE. My handsome Captain!! (*Raises her glass.*)

VERONIQUE. Sitting there over supper bragging about her fancy boyfriend and her fabulous life style, in front of us, with our broken marriages and broken hearts.

MARIE CLARE. I love him now, I loved him then . . .

VERONIQUE. I've thought of a way to really, really, hurt her.

MARIE CLARE. I'll love him till I die . . .

VERONIQUE (*slaps sister*). Listen. She can only stay for a month, right, and if she's late, something awful happens back at casa el Beastini! So, we're really nice to her to make her think we're on her side, and when it's time for her to go back we say we really need her to stay and help us become better people, she extends her stay, she's late back to the palace and Beast features, finally, gets his mighty jaws a mashing into our dear little sis. It's a really, really, good idea!

MARIE CLARE. I'll love him . . . (*Baby crying.*) Oh, no!

VERONIQUE. Shut ya gob, you crying, smelly, vomiting, blob!

MARIE CLARE. From hell!

VERONIQUE. What's the point of babies!!!

MARIE CLARE. Absolutely, no idea!

BEAUTY *comes out rocking Madeleine, singing.*

BEAUTY.
Little Lamb, who made thee?
Dost thou know who made thee?
Gave thee life and bid thee feed,
By the stream and o'er the mead;
Gave thee clothing of delight,
Softest clothing, wooly, bright;
Gave thee such a tender voice,
Making all the vales rejoice?
Little Lamb who made thee?
Dost thou know who made thee?

VERONIQUE. You can keep her! If you like her so much!

MARIE CLARE (*aside*). I thought we were being nice to her?

VERONIQUE (*aside*). We'll start in the morning!

BEAUTY.
Little Lamb, I'll tell thee,
Little Lamb, I'll tell thee:
He is called by thy name,

For he calls himself a Lamb.
He is meek and he is mild;
He became a little child.
I a child and thou a lamb.
We are called by his name.
Little Lamb, God bless thee!
Little Lamb, God bless thee!

JEAN LOUIS. Out here, everybody.

BEAUTY. On the evening I was due to leave for the palace . . .

JEAN LOUIS. Drinks in the garden.

Enter FAMILY, *drinking and laughing,* BEAUTY *holding Maddy,* EMILE *with a number of ice cream lollipops.*

BEAUTY. We enjoyed another family meal. This time to say goodbye.

EMILE. Great news. I have created new technologies that make it possible for me to extract the essence of metals and precious stones . . .

ANDRE. Emile, not tonight.

EMILE. The flavour of rock and ocean and tree. Here we have, a curry and aluminium cornet with a coal dust coulis and a diamond-flavoured chocolate flake. A horse chestnut and emerald sorbet with a Pacific Ocean and leather handbag sauce . . .

VERONIQUE. Look shortie, no one wants anything to do with your vile concoctions.

MARIE CLARE. I'd like a scoop of vanilla with a nice little biscuit, please.

PHILLIPE. Family. I've been saving this bottle for a special occasion. You all know I've been engaged for rather a long time now. Well, today Genevieve and I set a date, we'll be married in the spring.

ANDRE. At last.

JEAN LOUIS. Phillipe and Genevieve! A glorious wedding. A long and happy marriage. Can't wait to get rid of you!

MARIE CLARE. I'm empty.

PHILLIPE. I just filled your glass.

ANDRE. You drink after the toast not before it.

ALL. Can't wait to get rid of you. (*They drink.*)

ANDRE. I'd also like to make an announcement. This is something I should have done a long time ago. I'm leaving you lot. I'm going to Paris to study astronomy!

PHILLIPE. At last, Andre.

JEAN LOUIS. Fill your glasses, everybody. To Andre. Astronomy. And Paris.

MARIE CLARE. I'm empty.

PHILLIPE. I just filled your glass.

ANDRE. You drink after the toast not before it.

JEAN LOUIS. Glad to see the back of you!

ALL. Glad to see the back of you. (*They drink.*)

VERONIQUE. And finally . . .

MARIE CLARE. Here. Here. (MARIE CLARE *empties her glass.*)

VERONIQUE. I haven't proposed the toast yet.

MARIE CLARE *fills her own. All filled.*

Tonight, we are due to bid farewell to our little sister.

MARIE CLARE. Good riddance to the vile monster . . .

VERONIQUE *bashes* MARIE CLARE *on bonce.*

VERONIQUE. But sis, I'm begging you, linger a little longer, be billeted in the bulging bosom of your loving family.

BEAUTY. I'm leaving at midnight.

ANDRE (*aside*). What's she up to?

VERONIQUE. We need you here, sis, you see, we've ruined our lives and you're the only one who can save us.

MARIE CLARE. We'll dance in her lungs . . .

VERONIQUE *whacks sister again.*

VERONIQUE. I play my cello upstairs in the attic at midnight weeping into my strings until I can't raise another note because I'm afraid of what's to become of me.

MARIE CLARE. We'll roast her eyes on a spit . . .

VERONIQUE *whacks sister again.*

VERONIQUE. Marie Clare gives ballet classes on Saturday mornings in the village hall to try and recapture some scraps of bliss from the precious time that was Paris.

MARIE CLARE. Drown her in the river like a kitten . . .

VERONIQUE *gags* MARIE CLARE *with hanky.*

VERONIQUE. I am, let's face it, a single parent, who can't even bring herself to like her own baby. Marie Clare is an adulteress and a drunk. But, we want to change and only you can help us. Show us a way out of the hell in which we live and the worse hell into which we may soon descend. Oh, we certainly wish we enjoyed some of the advantages you enjoy. The palace, a glorious home, the Beast, a rich and powerful fiancé. You see, we are the unlucky ones, ghosts who want to live, give us back our lives, thorns that long to be roses, so prune us, we are sick and want to be well again, help heal us. And think what might happen to little Maddy without her auntie to look after her.

BEAUTY. I'll stay.

VERONIQUE. Promise.

BEAUTY. Just for a few days.

VERONIQUE. That will be quite long enough.

Midnight. 'BEAUTY' *spoken.*

BEAUTY. Beast.

VERONIQUE. Sis! So . . . glad you're staying.

Raises a glass. MARIE CLARE *falls over.*

ALL. So glad!!

ANDRE (*aside*). She's up to something.

Toast. All sleep. Music.

BEAUTY. In the days that followed, I could never find Veronique and Marie Clare to have our important conversations.

BOYS. Don't trust them, Beauty . . .

BEAUTY. All our arrangements to meet, mysteriously, misfired . . .

WITCH. They are not on your side, Beauty!

BEAUTY. They were full of apologies and had the most plausible excuses . . .

ALL. Beauty!

BEAUTY. But . . . I was left feeling . . . frustrated, and foolish, and angry!

ALL. Your promise!

BEAUTY. I was beginning to realise that I was being played for a fool.

ALL. Beast needs you.

BEAUTY. I'm coming.

ALL. Come home. Beast is dying.

BEAUTY. No! (*Sings.*)
Over land, any land,
Over sea, any sea,
Take me where my heart must be.

ALL. Over land.
Over sea.
Any land. Any sea.
Take me where heart must be.
Heart must be. Free.
Heart must be. Free.

WITCH *gestures. Dream dissolves into hurricane. Furniture and props thrown into a whirlwind. All exit but* BEAUTY.

Scene Four: Victory

BEAUTY. I'm home!

Music. Enter BEAST, WITCH, CHORUS.

WITCH. She's here now, Beast.

WITCH *guides* BEAST*'s hand to* BEAUTY. *They touch.*

BEAST. Home.

BEAUTY (*rubbing* BEAST*'s hand*). Home. I'm sorry I'm late. I let myself be deceived.

BEAST. All. Make. Mistakes.

BEAUTY. I failed you!

BEAST. All. Fail.

BEAUTY. I broke my word!

BEAST. Be, not . . . discouraged.

BEAST *staggers.* WITCH *checks his pulse.*

WITCH. I have no magic that can save him. (WITCH *moves away.*)

BEAUTY (*lifts* BEAST *in her arms*). No words, till then. Do you remember? No words. At supper on my first day in the palace, we agreed not to speak of marriage until the day I could put my hand on my heart and know that it was full of love and full of joy. Do you remember? (*Lifts a hand. Very frail.*) Well, my heart is full of love and full of joy and without fear and without pity, I accept your proposal, I will be your wife.

WITCH. The curse is broken!

Music. BEAST *transforms into* PRINCE. *During transformation* WITCH *and* CHORUS *strip* BEAST*, which gives him the kiss of life. The* PRINCE *stands. He staggers and falls like a foal. When he is steady on his feet he is dressed by the* CHORUS*, given a sword and cloak as befits a prince.*

ALL. Sickness will make him strong.
Suffering will make him good.
Cruelty will make him kind.
And pain will make him wise.

PRINCE. Heart. Full . . .

BEAUTY. Of love.

PRINCE: Heart. Full . . .

BEAUTY. Of joy.

BEAST. I was the Beast and now I am free. (*They embrace.*)

ALL (*sing*).
Beauty.
Beauty.
Beauty.
See, with more than your eyes.
See, with more than your eyes.
See, with more than your eyes.

PRINCE. Witch, who did this to me?

WITCH. Ezmeralda cursed you!

PRINCE. Who is Ezmeralda?

WITCH (*holding something, in her hands*). A witch, who used her powers for evil and not for good.

PRINCE. Show me.

WITCH *hands* the PRINCE *the words of his curse. Music.*

Let the boy live in perpetual pain.
Let him disnatured be and live half-man half-beast
And to repel all human kind let him
Bear the name of cannibal though he be none.

(In growing anger.) Why did she bury me in hell!!

WITCH. She looked into your cot and fell in love with you, as you grew, her love grew deeper and disguised as a nurse and then as a tutor she lived beside you for eighteen years, on the day you came to manhood, it was declared that you'd leave home to seek a wife and see the world and Esmeralda, terrified at the thought of losing you turned herself into a Princess and asked for your hand, when you refused her, so that you could never leave her and so that no other woman could have what she loved most, she put that curse upon you.

PRINCE. I'll cut her in pieces, with my sword!!

WITCH. When Beast was born, Esmeralda believed she'd find peace, her Prince dependent on her and in a shape to repel all rivals, but even as Beast's birth blood dried on her hands, the cold, clear waters of repentance fell on her cheeks and appalled at the horror of her curse and employing all the magic in her power she tried to blast you out of the torment into which she'd cast you. But her curse could not be broken quickly or by blatant force. (WITCH *holding another container, she's very nervous now.*)

PRINCE. What's that?

WITCH. The words of Ezmeralda's antidote.

PRINCE. Let me read!

WITCH. Here.

Music.

PRINCE (*reads*).
When a maiden shall choose to marry this monster,
Freely choose in joy and love and without pity
Innocent of my curse and of its cure
Then will the evil end, then will the Prince be free.
With this, you two saved my life.

WITCH. Prince. I am Esmeralda. The curse was mine.

PRINCE *advances on her with his sword.* WITCH *kneels.*

Your sword will bring me peace.

PRINCE. You, cursed me?

BEAUTY. She cursed you and then she gave her life to save you!

PRINCE (*sword still drawn*). Witch. (*Raises his sword. Music.*)

WITCH. I deserve to die.

PRINCE. Your crime against me was monstrous but your death would restore nothing that has been lost. You worked selflessly to free me from your curse. Stand up. You are free.

WITCH. I am not worthy.

ALL (*sing*)
Sickness will make him strong.
Suffering will make him good.
Cruelty will make him kind.
And pain will make him wise.

PRINCE. Witch, let me ask one last favour before you go?

WITCH. Speak.

PRINCE. Will you bring Beauty's family to our wedding.

WITCH. Beauty!?

BEAUTY. Erm. Well. Okay.

Music. WITCH *stands,* BEAUTY *and* PHILLIPE *sing and spin.*

ALL. To the East of the Sun, to the West of the moon. Beauty's family in this room. East. West. Sun. Moon. Beauty's family to this room.

FAMILY *transform and tumble into action.*

ANDRE. Was that some kind of kinetic, super gravitational force, Beauty? (*He falls over.* CHORUS *assist.*)

MARIE CLARE. We were at the hairdresser's.

GIRLS *upside down, legs cycling.*

VERONIQUE. It's completely inconvenient, Beauty.

BEAUTY. Papa!

BEAUTY *rushes to* JEAN LOUIS, *lifts him up, embraces him.*

EMILE. Who fancies a stick of candy floss? (*Has it with him.*)

BEAUTY. What, no ice cream, Emile?

EMILE. I've moved on sister. Now I make all kinds of confectionery, in the current climate, you can't put all your eggs in one basket.

EMILE *is about to hand him a stick.*

PRINCE. I'd love to try some.

BEAUTY. What flavour is that?

EMILE. Lobster claws and baked ankle bracelet. Sprinkled with a little chewing gum and cow's udder sauce.

PRINCE. Oh!?

EMILE. I'm getting more middle of the road, you see, to appeal to the family market, I can't keep living in that bunker, sister. Did you try it yet?

PRINCE. Er. No. (*Bites.*) It's good. It's really, really good.

JEAN LOUIS. Beauty. Where's Beast?

BEAUTY. And so Beauty told her family the whole story!

FAMILY. Wow!

BEAUTY. Her brothers were amazed.

BROTHERS *all in a dead faint at once.*

Her sisters were delighted.

VERONIQUE. Oh, sis! To meet a Prince, at last!! Let's do it!!

MARIE CLARE. Bonjour, dread liege! Enchanté!

VERONIQUE. Oh, oh! Something grovelling! And witty! In French!

BEAUTY. Papa, this man wants to be my husband.

PRINCE. Do I have permission to marry your daughter, sir?

JEAN LOUIS. With all my heart.

Music. A dance. At the climax. VERONIQUE *and* MARIE CLARE *grab* BEAUTY.

VERONIQUE (*to the musos*). Stop, that awful folksy racket, you pot-bellied, beardies.

PHILLIPE *lunges in.*

And you lot stay back or blob gets it.

MARIE CLARE. Yeah. Right.

VERONIQUE. If you think we're gonna stand by and let this selfish little starlet, kop for lots of cash, marry a hunky Prince and live . . .

VERONIQUE. happily ever after, you've got another think coming.

MARIE CLARE. Totally! What she said!

VERONIQUE. So! Witch woman, you seem to be pretty handy with the old magic tricks, magic me and my sis a big palace, stuffed to the gills with pots of gold, posh servants, expensive frocks and . . .

MARIE CLARE. And him!! (*She is pointing vigorously at the* PRINCE.)

VERONIQUE. Yeah. And throw in the hunky Prince! Can you sort that? 'Cause if you can't, blob gets a really, really sore throat.

MARIE CLARE. Yeah! So, do it, sister!

VERONIQUE. Do the magic thing, witch woman!

WITCH. Bear with me while I wind up a spell.

VERONIQUE. And no tricks, right?

WITCH. No tricks, sister.

Music. WITCH *spells,* CHORUS *dance.* SISTERS *frozen.*

WITCH. For you two, there'll be no happy end, you've been turned into statues by a witch. You can still hear and see and feel, but you'll remain frozen in stone, watching Beauty's happiness, until you empty your hearts of vanity, envy, spite and pride. Don't wait too long. Farewell.

BEAUTY. You're leaving?

WITCH. My work is done.

BEAUTY. If we need you?

WITCH. Seek me.

BEAUTY. Where?

WITCH. In silence! At which point, to avoid protracted and sentimental goodbyes, the witch turned herself into a raven. And flew. To another place . . .

PRINCE. We must return to the world of mankind.

BEAUTY. There is much work to be done.

Song of Joy.

BEAUTY.
It is right it should be so,
That man is made for joy and woe,
And when this we rightly know
Thro' the world we safely go.

ALL. Know this and safely go.

BEAUTY. Joy and woe are woven fine,
Clothing for the soul divine
Under every grief and pine.
Runs a joy with silken twine.

ALL. Know this and safely go.

They wrap themselves up against the elements and begin the long journey back to the material world, BROTHERS *carrying* SISTERS.